A PER[illegible] TO
HODG[illegible]
FOR STO[illegible]
STRAIGH[illegible]
HISTORICAL GRAPEV[illegible]

1. How did Isadora Duncan die?
2. What was George Bernard Shaw's view of drinking?
3. What was Salvador Dali's reaction when offered a raw oyster for the first time?
4. What were actor Edmund Gwenn's last words?
5. Who said: "Nature gives you the face you have at twenty. Life shapes the face you have at thirty. But at fifty you get the face you deserve"?

The answers are in
HODGEPODGE

"Readers of this delightful compilation of offbeat facts, colorful anecdotes, frequently hilarious quotations, and wry observations need never face the embarrassment of a 'flagging conversation.' Bryan has supplied them with a wealth of surefire conversation resuscitators. He is a reliable and sprightly guide to the bizarre, the bawdy and the belly-busting. Recommended for dipping into whenever the spirits need a boost."

The Kirkus Reviews

HODGEPODGE

A Commonplace Book

J. Bryan, III

BALLANTINE BOOKS • NEW YORK

 Published in the United States of America by Ballantine Books, a division of Random House, Inc., New York, and simultaneously in Canada by Random House of Canada Limited, Toronto.

Library of Congress Catalog Card Number: 86-47659

ISBN 0-345-34204-6

This edition published by arrangement with Atheneum Publishers, a division of The Scribner Book Companies, Inc.

Manufactured in the United States of America

First Ballantine Books Edition: October 1987

For my ouaffe,
from her oosbon

How these curiosities would be quite forgott, did not such idle fellowes as I putt them down.

JOHN AUBREY

This is a volume which it will be found exceedingly easy to leave alone.

FREDERICK LOCKER-LAMPSON
My Confidences

Foreword

The first time I met the term was in "The Adventure of the Missing Three-Quarter," when Sherlock Holmes "stretched out his hand and took down . . . his commonplace book." In my vocabulary, *commonplace* meant "trite" or "ordinary," and because nothing about the exotic Holmes could possibly be either, I went to the dictionary. There it was: "A book containing memoranda of passages or events for reference." I never saw Holmes's commonplace book, of course, but I have now read Robert Southey's and W. H. Auden's, which so fascinated me that I decided to compile one of my own. *Hodgepodge* is it.

The title might quite as well have been *Potpourri* or *Gallimaufry* or *Salmagundi* or *Olla-podrida*, or *Canapés* or *Snacks* or *Chowchow* or even *Hash*. Any word suggesting a miscellany would do, because that is what this book is: a miscellaneous collection of oddities and curiosities, anecdotes, idle thoughts, quips and quizzes, unusual incidents, and bits of doggerel that have caught my attention over years of quaquaversal reading and travel. It is a book for dipping and skipping, suitable for bedside or loo-side, not one that demands sustained attention. I have put all these items together chiefly for my own amusement (as when I find a slot for *quaquaversal*), but if, as I hope, I happen to amuse the reader too, so much the better.

Finally, a word of apology and explanation:

My notes for some of the items which follow were hastily scribbled on the back of envelopes and such. When I reviewed them for transcription, I was daunted by their occasional illegibility and dismayed by their sketchiness—dates, identifications and even sources were often lacking. I have filled in the gaps as best I could, but some remain; e.g., who was Beauterne, to whom Napoleon made a startling remark? (See page 214.) For these and other flaws, I beg the reader's indulgence.

J. Bryan, III

BROOK HILL
RICHMOND, VA. 23227

Contents

Absent-Mindedness

I never met anyone so absent-minded as Proessor Sylvester, the great mathematician. One afternoon, just as I was going for a walk, he handed me an ink-bottle, begging me to drop it in the letter-box, as he was anxious to have an immediate answer.

HENRIETTA CORKRAN, *Celebrities and I*

Aunt Dosia, who married a parson, retained a faint beauty in her old age, but her wits wilted. Once at the Easter Communion, when her husband handed her the full chalice, she drained it to the last drop, murmuring "perfectly delicious," and handed it back in the presence of the whole congregation.

SHANE LESLIE, *Long Shadows*

Florence Lascelles [daughter of the British ambassador to Germany] married Sir Cecil Spring-Rice—a very absent-minded man who came all the way from Stockholm to propose to her and only remembered why he had come as he was closing the Embassy Door! He had to go back again to ask for her hand.

H.R.H. PRINCESS ALICE, Countess of Athlone, *For My Grandchildren*

Miss Evans, the accomplished sister of the Provost [of Eton], once gave a dinner party and addressed all the invitations to one person. At a friend's dinner party, she forgot she was not in her own house, and was heard apologizing to a lady near her, "I can't tell you, my dear, how sorry I am that this dinner is a failure—I can never rely on my cook."

(MRS.) E. M. WARD, *Memories of 90 Years*

Canon Sawyer's splendid absent-mindedness once led him, while welcoming a visitor at the railway station, to board the departing train and disappear.

New Statesman

His mind is somewhat too much taken up with his mind.

JOHN EARLE (1601?–65), "The Down-Right Scholar," in *Microcosmography; or, a Piece of the World Discovered*

A certain (or rather *un*certain) French hostess introduced a Señor de Castro as "Señor Circumcisio." And a New York hostess, giving a dinner for Prince Yussupov, who helped murder Rasputin, introduced him to her other guests as "Prince Rasputin, who murdered—Just who was it you *did* murder, Prince Rasputin?"

I myself am so absent-minded and forgetful that my roster of friends has been reduced to What's His Name, and my vocabulary of common nouns to Thingumajig and What You May Call It.

Spooner of Oxford, celebrated for his absence of mind, was one evening found wandering disconsolately about the streets of Greenwich. "I've been here for hours," he said. "I had an important appointment to meet someone at the Dull Man, Greenwich, and I can't find it anywhere; and the odd thing is that no one seems to have heard of it." Late at night he went back to Oxford. "You idiot!" exclaimed his wife; "Why, it was the Green Man, Dulwich, you had to go to."

AUGUSTUS J. C. HARE, *The Story of My Life*

I once went to a dinner party in Ardmore, Pennsylvania, at which the host, instead of saying grace, recited his telephone number and ended "Amen!"

"The horror of that moment," the King [of Hearts] went on, "I shall never, *never* forget!"

"You will, though," the Queen said, "if you don't make a memorandum of it."

LEWIS CARROLL, *Through the Looking Glass*

Mr. George Harvest, minister of Thames Ditton, was one of the most absent-minded men of his time—so much so, indeed, that he frequently used to forget the prayer days and to walk to church with his gun to see what could have assembled the people there. One day Lady Onslow, being desirous of knowing something of the most remarkable planets and constellations, requested Mr. Harvest, on a fine starlight night, to point them out to her, which he undertook to do; but in the midst of his lecture, having occasion to make water, thought this need not interrupt it, and accordingly directed that operation with one hand, and went on in his explanation, pointing out the constellations with the other.

FRANCIS GROSE, *The Olio* (1796)

A well-known conductor was taking the orchestra through a symphony when the first violin managed to indicate with his bow that the conductor's fly buttons were undone. Hastily he turned his back on the orchestra, and buttoned himself up. In front of an audience of 5,000 people.

MICHAEL BATEMAN, in the *Sunday Times* of London

On a trip to Israel, Professor Arthur Goodhart, the eminent ex-Master of University College, Oxford, was asked by airport authorities how he traveled. Instead of replying, "By El Al," the Israeli airline, he said, "By Al Fatah," the Arab guerilla organization. The officials took him aside for further questions.

Jewish Chronicle

Voltaire began a passionate letter "My dear Hortense—" and ended it "Farewell, my dear Adèle!"

Sir John Gielgud is notorious for both his absent-mindedness and his tactless remarks. He and E——K——were chatting about a mutual friend when Gielgud observed, "I know, but he's such a *bore*! He's almost as big a bore as E——K——!"

RONALD HAYMAN, *Saturday Times Review*

Max Schodl, an Austrian painter, hopped into a cab and told the driver, "Number six! I'll tell you the street in a moment."

Actors and Actresses

A friend of mine did a play for Miss [Mary] Eastlake [1856–1911]. At rehearsal he noticed that in Act Two she entered, drying her eyes with a handkerchief. To his inquiries, she explained that the curtain of Act One had left her weeping. When he pointed out that fifteen years were supposed to elapse between the two acts, Miss Eastlake argued that mere passing of time made no difference: the audience, having seen her in tears, would expect to discover traces of distress when she came on next. Miss Eastlake had her own way.

W. PETT RIDGE, *A Story Teller*

Ellen Terry had a large green umbrella which she called "Miss Toosey."

HENRIETTE CORKRAN, *Celebrities and I*

I have never heard a dull story about an actor, a parrot or a Negro preacher.

ARTHUR KROCK

Mary Anderson, known a century ago as "the queen of the American stage," spent her childhood in Louisville, Ky. It was there that she conceived her ambition to become an actress; and her autobiography, *A Few Memories*, tells how she began training herself for the role of Juliet: "To get the hollow tones of her voice in the tomb, and better realize my heroine's feelings on awakening in her 'nest of death, contagion, and unnatural sleep,' I frequently walked to Cave Hill, Louisville's beautiful cemetery, here to speak her lines through the grilled door of a vault."

(When Miss Anderson was acting in London, she used to go to a nearby church between the matinée and evening performances and pray "to be spared the attentions of the King," Edward VII.)

John Barrymore, in derogation of Leslie Howard's rather anemic Hamlet: "When *I* stepped onstage as Hamlet, you could hear my balls *clank*!"

Comment on an admirably mannered actor: "He doesn't act; he behaves."

W. PETT RIDGE, *A Story Teller*

Mrs. Siddons was always acting. One night at dinner she turned to the footman and said in a theatrical tone, "Give me a glass of water, I pray you; I am athirst today."

AUGUSTUS J. C. HARE, *The Story of My Life*

An actor was appearing in court as a character-witness for a friend. The opposing attorney, trying to fluster and discredit him, asked whom he considered the handsomest man on the American stage.

The actor studied his fingernails for a moment, then answered, "Myself." The courtroom hooted.

Afterward, the friend protested, "How *could* you say a thing like that? You made a fool of yourself and made me ridiculous by association!"

The actor was contrite. "I know, my dear fellow! I *know*, and I'm terribly sorry! But you must remember, I was under oath."

More saints have been drawn from the acting profession than from any other. Among them are SS. Ardalion, Porphyry and Genesta.

[Sarah Bernhardt] once returned from a triumphant London engagement with a monkey named Darwin, a parrot named Bouzi-Bouzi, a cheetah and seven live chameleons on a gold chain about her neck.

CORNELIA OTIS SKINNER,
Elegant Wits and Grand Horizontals

I can't help recognizing that [the actress Theresa] is a superior artist—she is able to produce that little shiver across the back of your neck which only great actresses evoke.

Paris and the Arts, 1851–1896, from the *Goncourt Journal*

The leader of Rachel's claque wrote her in 1840: "We had three acclamations, four hilarities, two thrilling movements, four renewals of applause, and two indefinite explosions."

I guess I bothered Bert [his partner, Bert Yorke] at times. After one show, in Cleveland, when we had come off the stage, Bert followed me into the dressing room. He had a red nose on and a funny facial make-up, and was wearing a dirty street cleaner's helmet, a yellow Inverness, in the lapel of which he had a large sponge posing as a chrysanthemum, and on his hands he had red rubber gloves. He was wearing sailor pants with a watch fob that was the handle of a toilet chain; he had soiled spats over a pair of big shoes, and was carrying a cane, the ferrule of which reposed in a rubber plunger. Arrayed like a thrift shop come to life, he said, and I quote, "I ain't going to be no straight man for nobody!"

FRED ALLEN, *Much Ado About Me*

America, to British Eyes and Ears

An English colonel, retired, who ran a pension in Istanbul where I stayed one summer: "There's a city in America I've always wanted to see. I don't know why. Its name just appeals to me. See-tl. See-tl. Such a lovely name!" (Much lovelier than "Seattle.")

"Bill Scanlon talks as Englishmen expect every real American to talk." Here are some samples: "I felt like the morning after a bottle of Prohibition Hooch. . . . Look it here, you Bindlestiff! I threw the chief high muck-a-muck down on his ear-hole. . . ."

SIR ARTHUR CONAN DOYLE, *The Maracot Deep*

I was introduced to Mrs. [Julia Ward] Howe, who wrote the hymn singing which the troops took Pittsburg *[sic]*.

AUGUSTUS J. C. HARE, *The Story of My Life*

Mr. Wilbraham said he had asked an American at Florence what he thought of the Venus de Medicis. "Wal, I guess I'm not so partiklar overpowered by stone gals," was the reply.

IB.

(The American's name was probably Silas Q. Corntossel, and surely he didn't say, "Wal, I guess," but "Wal, I calc'late ez haow. . . .")

An Englishman to Harry Cooper, proudly: "I can name quite a number of your states: New York, Florida, California, Susquehanna. . . ."

Another Englishman, to Corey Ford: "What state is New Hampshire in?"

Corey (who lived there): "Terrible!"

And one to my father, in Cairo: "From Virginia, eh? Then perhaps you know my brother in Montana?"

And one to Marty Sommers in Paris: "Tell me, how should I pronounce it: 'I-o-way' or 'O-hee-o'?"

Capone opened a drawer and counted fifty "grands" onto his desk top.

EGON LARSON, *The Deceivers*

He would call on his friend in the latter's home town on Rhode Island in a fortnight's time.

IB.

[An American speaking:] "I was raised in a ten-cent fish joint. . . . They tell me that in this country [i.e., England] you don't get the hot squat, not without you earn it good and plenty. . . . She passed in her checks very, very sudden. . . . She was there and cracking hardy. . . . It excited him about as much as a raspberry drink at a departmental store. . . . I reckon he'll want to know the how-to about those bonds. He's a wise coon. . . . Well, ain't you the clam's cuticle!"

NGAIO MARSH, *Death in Ecstasy*

Lord Asquith [Prime Minister, 1908–16] turned to me at dinner and said, "Tell me, Ethel, have you ever heard of an American named Alexander Hamilton?"

ETHEL BARRYMORE, *Memories*

Art and Artists

What are the correct, formal titles of the paintings known as (1) *Whistler's Mother* and (2) *Gainsborough's Blue Boy* and of (3) the statue known as "Eros," at the center of Picadilly Circus? Answers at the end of this section.

Edwin Landseer...was the greatest animal painter that ever lived....He was the most delightful story-teller, and the most charming companion in the world. He also sang delightfully....I once heard him [say], "If people only knew as much about painting as I do, they would never buy my pictures."

W. P. FRITH, *My Autobiography and Reminiscences*

Sir Joshua Reynolds's sister was also an artist. It was said of her pictures that "they made her brother cry and everyone else laugh."

Cézanne worked very slowly. His friend, the famous art dealer Ambroise Vollard, underwent no fewer than 115 sittings for a single portrait. Cézanne commented, "I am not entirely displeased with the shirt front."

Compton's Encyclopedia

Sir Frederick Taylor, the President of the Water-Color Society, once saw in a shop "a framed engraving of his own well-known picture of *The Weighing of the Deer*, but there was an inscription over it describing it as 'This fine engraving after Landseer.' The shopman was standing in the doorway, and Sir Frederick said to him, 'That picture is not

Landseer's,' on which the man retorted, 'Just you talk about what you understand!' "

HENRY HOLIDAY, *Reminiscences of My Life*

Art is the power of creating organisms out of stone, clay, colours, tones, words.

SCHUMACHER, *Handbuch der Architektur*

Until the end of the nineteenth century, men visiting the Hermitage Museum in St. Petersburg were expected to wear white tie and tails.

Protogenes spent 7 years over one picture, sharpening his sensitivity by eating only bread crust dipped in water.

MAURICE RHEIMS, *The Strange Life of Objects*

[In 1689, two lay Jesuits, Belleville, a Frenchman, and Gherardini, an Italian, were established in the palace of the Emperor K'ang Hsi, to paint portraits and decoration of various kinds.] One day when Gherardini had finished a large architectural picture in which were columns that appeared to recede in perspective, the Chinese were at first sight stupefied and believed that he had used some magic art to produce the effect. Even upon approaching the canvas they were scarcely convinced by the touch that it was a visual deception upon a flat surface. Then they cried out: "There is nothing more contrary to nature than to represent distances where there are actually none or where they cannot be."

J. A. LLOYD HYDE, *Oriental Lowestoft*

The Common Man always likes minute detail in pictures. Turner was attacked even when young for not "finishing" his works.

RAYMOND MORTIMER, in the *Sunday Times* of London

A convention in equestrian statuary requires the horse to be standing on all four feet if the rider is a national hero; on three feet, if the rider died from wounds received in battle; on two feet, if he was killed in battle.

Upon the problem of St. Peter's were engaged the minds of Bramante, Michael Angelo, Raphael, Peruzzi, Sangallo, Fontana, Maderna and Bernini. So much originality could not, without peril, be focused at a single point.

GEOFFREY SCOTT, *The Architecture of Humanism*

Vasari mentioned crimson in Mona Lisa's lips and cheeks, now lost to us.

E. V. LUCAS, *A Wanderer in Paris*

Vlaminck's "Bouquet de Fleurs" sold for 600 francs in 1920, 500,000 in 1950, 5,000,000 in 1959.

IB.

John Henry Fuseli (1741–1825), who painted *The Nightmare* and other bloodcurdlers, was not an Italian, as I long thought, but a Swiss; nor is the correct pronunciation of his name "Few-*zel*-li," but "*Fewz*-li."

Even grimmer than Fuseli was Antoine Wiertz (1806–65) of Belgium—grimmer and more strange. Here, for example, are three of his titles: *Thoughts and Visions of a Severed Head, Premature Burial* and *One Second after Death.* (Note here Leigh Hunt's observation in "The Countenance After Death": "A corpse seems as if it suddenly knew everything, and was profoundly at peace in consequence.") Even stranger, some of Wiertz's canvases are large enough to roof a tennis court. Strangest of all, he wouldn't sell them. They are on view in his old studio, now the Musée Wiertz, in Brussels. (Fuseli and Wiertz should have illustrated Poe.)

The original name of Bernard Berenson, the great contemporary authority on art, was Bernhard Valvrojenski.

. . . this age, when studies of still life are apparently composed on moving easels with semi-explosive paints.

SIR SHANE LESLIE

Constable observed a landscape so intently and quietly that, while he sat, a field-mouse entered his coat-pocket and fell asleep there.

C. R. LESLIE, *Memoirs of the Life of John Constable*

Whistler . . . standing upright, immaculate, dainty, doing little watercolors as another man would roll a cigarette.

EDWARD MARSH, *A Number of People*

In the ancient mosaics in St. Mark's, Venice, the Pyramids appear in the background of a Joseph-subject to show that it is Egypt; . . . the Pyramids have windows, which is not quite correct, but it was the best they knew.

HENRY HOLIDAY, *Reminiscences of My Life*

According to Agnolo Firenzuola, the slight openings at the corners of Mona Lisa's mouth, where her lips do not quite close, were considered by her sixteenth-century contemporaries as evidence of elegance and lofty birth.

[A fault in the canvas of his painting *Triumph of the Innocents* continued to give Holman Hunt trouble.] Working late one night alone in his studio, he believed he had finally cured it, and muttered to himself, "I think I have beaten the devil." Whereupon the building shook with a great convulsion, and some enormous thing appeared to hurl itself towards the door from a spot immediately behind the easel. Hunt's sense of symbolic significance didn't let him down. The faulty patch was where he had been trying to complete the heads of the Christ-child and the Virgin Mary, and it was 1:30 on Christmas morning.

Sunday Times of London

... those great Italian primitives exported by American collectors after the war [were] covered by atrocious "modern" paintings which the collector would then order his restorer in New York to scrape off, revealing the masterpiece beneath (thus evading customs at both the Italian and American ends). A well-founded tradition has it that one such collector, after some delay, sent his restorer a worried telegram: HOW ARE YOU GETTING ON? The reply came back, HAVE REMOVED FUTURISTIC DAUB, SCRAPED OFF FAKE DUCCIO, AM DOWN TO PORTRAIT OF MUSSOLINI, WHERE DO I STOP?

HUGH VICKERS AND CAROLINE MCCULLOUGH,
Great Country House Disasters

(Answers)

1. *Arrangement in Black and Gray, No. 1.*
2. *Jonathan Buttall.*
3. *The Angel of Christian Charity.* This last is actually a monument to the philanthropic Earl of Shaftesbury. (It is made of aluminum, by the way.)

Astronomy

[Giuseppe] Piazzi's discovery [of the planet Ceres] has the stronger historical mark set upon it from the fact of its having been made on the first night of the nineteenth century.

SIR HENRY HOLLAND, *Recollections of a Past Life*

One evening the children came rushing in from the garden, very excited. "Come quickly, come quickly," was their urgent request. "The moon is wobbling!" The older generation smiled indulgently. We refused to be drawn from our comfortable positions and conversation. But the morning papers were full of an account of the moon having "oscillated perceptibly," an unprecedented event, as far as I know.

(MRS.) E. M. WARD, *Memories of 90 Years*

Dante, in *The Divine Comedy*, gives an exact description of the Southern Cross, a constellation which is invisible in the Northern hemisphere and which no traveller in those days could ever have seen. [Yet Dante incorrectly put Venus nearest the sun.] Swift, in *The Journey to Laputa*, gives the distances and periods of rotation of the two satellites of Mars, unknown at that time. When the American astronomer, Asaph Hall, discovered them in 1877 and noticed that his calculations corresponded to Swift's indications, he was seized with a sort of panic and named them *Phobos* and *Deimos*: "Fear" and "Terror."

LOUIS PAUWELS AND JACQUES BERGIER,
The Morning of the Magicians

Venus is the only planet that rotates from east to west.

Barroom Bets

(ANSWERS ON NEXT PAGE)

1. Each of two persons takes a well-shuffled pack of playing cards and turns up one card at a time, keeping pace. When they have gone through the packs completely, what are the chances that both will have simultaneously turned up identical cards (i.e., same suit, same denomination)?
2. When is the first day of the twenty-first century?
3. In what moving picture did Humphrey Bogart say, "Play it again, Sam!"?
4. If you straighten out a standard paper clip, how long is the wire, within ½ inch?
5. On a locomotive running from New York to Chicago, is any part of it moving toward New York?
6. A house is being moved on rollers which are exactly five feet in circumference. For every complete revolution of the rollers, how far forward does the house move?
7. Imagine a free-running pulley with a rope through it. On one end of the rope is a weight of 150 pounds; on the other, a sailor weighing exactly 150 pounds. As the sailor climbs the rope, does the weight go up or down or stay at the same level?
8. Mark Twain was born in Florida. True or false?
9. Cornwallis did not surrender at Yorktown. True or false?
10. Given two glasses of equal volume, one exactly half full of wine, the other exactly half full of water. Stir one teaspoonful of the wine into the water glass, then stir one teaspoonful of the mixture into the wineglass. Question: Is the proportion of wine to water in the first glass greater than, less than, or equal to the proportion of water to wine in the second glass?

BARROOM BETS *(Answers)*

1. Five times in eight. Try it!
2. January 1, 2001. The present century ends on December 31, 2000.
3. None. What he said in *Casablanca* was: "If she can stand it, I can. Play it."
4. Four inches.
5. Yes, the part of the wheel flanges below the rail.
6. Ten feet.
7. It goes up.
8. True. He was born in the small town of Florida, Missouri.
9. True. Cornwallis pled illness, and Maj. Gen. Charles O'Hara surrendered for him.
10. They are equal.

The Bible

The Book of Esther is the only one that does not mention God.

A strange non sequitur, in 1 Kings 15:23: "The rest of all the acts of Asa, and all his might, and all that he did, and the cities which he built, are they not written in the book of Chronicles of the Kings of Judah? Nevertheless in the time of his old age he was diseased in his feet."

"Nevertheless"?

A ranting Irish preacher, who lost himself completely in the mazes of his own nonsense, finally made us laugh by the emphasis with which he announced, "As it is written, my brethren, in the Duke of Bookeronomy—."

AUGUSTUS J. C. HARE, *The Story of My Life*

2 Kings 19 and Isaiah 37 are almost identical.

The complete text of the Bible contains 773,692 words, which themselves contain 3,566,480 letters.

I once heard a missionary describe the extraordinary difficulty he had found in translating the Bible into Eskimo. It was useless to talk of corn or wine to a people who did not know what they meant, so he had to use equivalents within their powers of comprehension. Thus in the Eskimo version of the Scriptures the miracle of Cana of Galilee is described as turning the water into *blubber*; the 8th verse of the 5th chapter of the First Epistle of St. Peter ran: "Your adversary the devil, as a roaring polar bear walketh about, seeking whom he may devour." In the same way "A land flowing with milk and honey" became "A land flowing with whale's blubber," and throughout the New Testament the words "Lamb of God" had to be translated "Little Seal of God. . . ." The missionary added that his converts had the lowest possible estimate of Jonah for not having utilized his exceptional opportunities by killing and eating the whale.

LORD FREDERIC HAMILTON,
The Days Before Yesterday

The last book in the Bible is often spoken of as "Revelations." Its correct name is Revelation—in full, The Revelation of Saint John the Divine.

Contrary to popular belief and to the song which says, "I saw Absalom a-hanging by his hair," he hung not by his hair but by his neck. Cf. 2 Samuel 18:9: "Absalom rode upon a mule, and the mule went under the thick boughs of a great oak, and his head caught hold of the oak, and he was taken up between the heaven and the earth."

Helpmeet is not a legitimate word, but a corruption that derives from Genesis 2:18, in which the Lord says of Adam, "It is not good that man should be alone; I will make an help meet [i.e., suitable] for him."

[Psalm 23, from *The Bible in Braid Scots*:]

The Lord is my Shepherd; my wants are a' kent; the pasture I lie on is growthie and green.

I follow by the lip o' the watirs o' Peace.

He heals and sterklie hauds my saul; amd airts me, for his ain name's sake, in a' the fit-roads o' his holiness.

Aye, and though I bude gang throwe the howe whaur the deid-shadows fa', I'se fear nae skaith nor ill, for that yersel is aye aside me; yere rod and yere cruik they defend me.

My table ye hae plenish't afore the een o' my faes; my heid ye hae chrystit wi' oyle; my cup is teemin fu!

And certes, tenderness and mercie sal be my fa' to the

end o' my days; and syne I'se bide i' the hoose o' the Lord, for evir and evir mair!

If I'd been challenged to guess how many parables there are in the Bible, I'd have said a dozen or perhaps fifteen. There are actually sixty-four.

St. Matthew 16:15—"He saith unto them, But whom say ye that I am?"—is not grammatical.

Colors

Green is the favorite color of snakes and other reptiles.

For every color-blind woman, there are twenty color-blind men.

In France, a yellow necktie indicates that the wearer is a wittol—a knowing cuckold—and a sardonic laugh is called "a yellow laugh."

Blue and green are the colors of the heavens, the sea, the shadows of the southern noon, the evening, the remote mountains. They are *cold*.... Yellow and red are the *popular* colors, the colors of the crowd, of children, of women and savages.... Brown is the unrealest color... the one major color that does not exist in the rainbow. A pure brown light is outside the possibilities of the Nature that we know.

OSWALD SPENGLER, *The Decline of the West*

Pink is India's navy blue.

DIANA VREELAND

In Russian, the word *krasnya* means both "red" and "beautiful."

Blue is the color of the Virgin; her robe is always blue.

Yellow is the color of jealousy, although the adjective usually attached to jealousy is "green-eyed."

Gargantua's colors were white and blue, by which his father wished it understood that it was a heavenly joy to him. For white signified to him pleasure, delights and rejoicing; and blue, celestial things.

RABELAIS

Every vowel in French has a special color: A black, E white, I red, U green, O blue.

ARTHUR RIMBAUD

Purple is the imperial color.

Some colors take their names from places—for instance, Prussian blue and French blue, Nile green, Pompeian red, Chinese white, Tyrian purple. Two others are less obvious, gamboge, from Cambodia, where the trees that produce the yellow powder are grown; and magenta, which commemorates Napoleon III's victory over the Austrians at Magenta, Italy, in 1859, about the time that the dye was discovered.

Mauve is pink trying to be purple.

WHISTLER

Men in a state of nature, uncilivized nations, children, have a great fondness for colors in their utmost brightness, and especially for yellow-red.

GOETHE, *Theory of Colors*

Among colors there are certain friendships, for some joined to others impart handsomeness and grace to them. When red is next to green or blue, they render each other more handsome and vivid. White, not only next to green or yellow, but next to almost any color, will add cheerfulness.

Dark colors among light ones look handsome, and so light ones look pretty among dark ones.

ALBERTI (1404–72)

When we were children words were colored
(Harlot and murder were dark purple).

LOUIS MACNEICE

Conversation

A person skilled in table talk is a *deipnosophist*.

If you ever have to support a flagging conversation, introduce the subject of eating.

LEIGH HUNT

Two other unfailing topics are said to be fires and servants. I myself would add superstitions and psychic experiences —and possibly the composition of the ideal dinner table. Virginia Faulkner (who wrote *Princess Tulip Murphy* and other delightful novels) had two more: "I ask the gentleman on my right, 'Are you a bed-wetter?', and when we have exhausted that, I remark to the gentleman on my left, 'You know, I spit blood this morning.' "

"Make a remark," said the Red Queen, "it's ridiculous to leave all the conversation to the pudding."

LEWIS CARROLL, *Through the Looking Glass*

The sixteenth Duke of Norfolk was heard to turn to a lady guest on his right and say, "I have only two topics of conversation—cricket and drains. Choose."

BRIAN MASTERS, *The Dukes*

Ming . . . had the advantage of his literary abilities, which enabled him to converse for an indefinite time upon a subject without expressing himself in any way about it, while Kwok Shen laboured under the necessity of having to achieve a specific issue.

ERNST BRAMAH, "Ming Tseun and the Emergency"

Topics absolutely taboo: suicide, money, operations, one's illustrious ancestors or connections, religion, incurable diseases, dreams, illegitimacy, bright sayings of one's children or grandchildren.

Jerry Wadsworth, in a final, desperate attempt to evoke a response from a lethargic dinner partner: "Do you like string?"

The Viceroy has a new trick to get him through the tedium of Indian dinner-parties. He turns to his female neighbour and asks, "If you were not a woman—what animal would you like to be?"

Chips: The Diaries of Sir Henry Channon

National Review ran a competition some years ago for the pair of remarks or questions judged most likely to kindle a conversation with a dinner partner. First prize went to "If you had your life to live over again, would you have come tonight?" and "Do you ever get the impression that Huntley and Brinkley can't stand each other?" My own favorites among the other entries were:

"Describe yourself in three simple declarative sentences."

"Is ground glass shiny after being cooked?" and

"Is it true that you are related to the hereditary King of Bohemia?"

If *National Review* ever sponsors another competition, here are my own two entries:

"Which do you think we will achieve first, communication with the dead or with animals?" and

"Which of these will be the greater benefit to mankind?"

Wilfred Blunt used to say that you could put ten per cent onto any story by making its leading figure a bishop.

EDWARD MARS, *A Number of People*

Henry James likened Holman Hunt's conversation to "a trickle of tepid water from a tap one is unable to turn off."

IB.

An indigestion is an excellent commonplace for two people that never met before.

WILLIAM HAZLITT, *Literary Remains*

The conversation of authors is not so good as might be imagined; but, such as it is (and with rare exceptions), it is better than any other.

IB., *Plain Speaker*

Table-talk, to be perfect, should be sincere without bigotry, differing without discord, sometimes grave, always agreeable, touching on deep points, dwelling most on seasonable ones, and letting everybody speak and be heard.

LEIGH HUNT, "Table-talk"

Avoid contradicting in general, especially people you love.

MAURICE BARING, *Have You Anything to Declare?*

Make not thy own Person, Family, Relations or Affairs, the frequent subject of thy Tattle. . . . Say not, in Truth, I cannot allow of such a thing. My Manner and Custom is to do thus. I neither eat nor drink in a morning. I am apt to be troubled with corns. My Child said such a Witty thing last night.

THOMAS FULLER, *Introductio ad Prudentiam*

When one is relating everything, interrupt him not, unless there be great reason for it: Don't say, No, it was thus, but I'll tell you. You leave out the best part of it, etc.

IB.

Underbrush words and phrases, to be trimmed out of one's conversation and thrown away: you might say, it seems to me, so to speak, in other words, as it were, as a matter of fact, you know, to put it another way, see?, okay?, unnastan?

Costumes and Fashions

The tuxedo, or dinner jacket, was introduced by Griswold Lorillard, of and at Tuxedo Park, N.Y., in 1886.

The sixth Nizam of Hyberabad never wore the same garment twice.

The buttons on the back of a tail coat, now vestigial, were put there originally to support a sword belt, and the buttons on the coat cuffs were to keep midshipmen from wiping their noses there.

The first Duke of Buckingham (1592–1628) wore a white velvet suit adorned with £70,000 worth of precious stones.

When one of King George V's courtiers ventured into his presence wearing trousers with turned-up cuffs, as was the new fashion, the king glared at them and remarked sourly, "I was not aware that my palace is damp."

The Duke of Windsor had his trousers made in London, and his jackets in New York. Beau Brummell went further: He, too, had different tailors for his jackets and trousers, but he also had a third, for his waistcoats. Moreover, he went to one glover for the thumbs and another for the rest of the hand.

The top hat originated as a crash helmet, a protection against concussion when the wearer fell on his head while fox hunting.

It is fearful to think of [King George IV] as Cyrus Redding saw him, "arrayed in deep-brown velvet, silver embroidered, with cut-steel buttons, and a gold net thrown over all." Before that "gold net thrown over all," the mistakes of his after-life seem to me to grow almost insignificant.

MAX BEERBOHM, "King George the Fourth"

By the time that the future King George IV was twenty-seven years old, he had run up a bill of £16,744 with his tailor alone.

A New York debutante, Mary Jacobs, invented (or at least patented) the brassiere, in 1914.

If prostitution is the oldest profession, the next oldest is tailoring. Before Adam became a gardener, he and Eve (cf. Genesis 3:7) "sewed fig leaves together, and made themselves aprons."

If people turn to look at you on the street, you are not well dressed.

BEAU BRUMMELL

The Crown Prince of Turkey, Yussuf Izzedine, considered it beneath his imperial dignity to be touched by an infidel, so the cutter [at his tailor's] had to take his measurements from a distance, without touching him. Yussuf also refused to wear the same pair of shoes more than once.

NUBAR GULBENKIAN, *Pantaraxia*

Benjamin Disraeli (1804–81) visited Malta in his mid-twenties and strolled around in a bloodred shirt with silver studs as big as shillings, an immense scarf for a girdle, stuffed with pistols and daggers, a broad blue-striped jacket and trousers, and a red cap and red slippers. Later, back in London (according to James Laver's *Dandies*), he appeared in "a black velvet suit with ruffles and black stockings with red clocks." Still later he dressed in "green velvet trousers, a canary coloured waistcoat, low shoes, silver buckles, lace at his wrists." On other occasions, "he wore purple trousers with a gold stripe down the seam, a scarlet waistcoat, gold chains and a profusion of rings (he even wore rings over his white gloves)." Until the publication of Bulwer-Lytton's novel *Pelham*, in 1828, tail coats were either dark blue or dark plum, but such was the influence of the fictional dandy Pelham that evening coats have been black ever since.

Adapted from *Dandies*

The Duke of Windsor invented the backless white waistcoat for wear with a dinner jacket, but it was his brother the Duke of Kent who invented the "Windsor knot" for four-in-hand ties.

In each ear commonly [the Indians of the Sasquesahannock tribe] have three great holes. . . . Some of their men wear in these holes, a small green and yellow colored snake, near half a yard in length, while crawling and lapping itself about his neck oftentimes familiarly would kiss his lips. Others wore a dead rat tied by the tail.

CAPTAIN JOHN SMITH,
The General History of Virginia

When Grand Duchess Marie of Russia, Czar Alexander II's only daughter, married Prince Alfred Duke of Edinburgh, she astonished his mother Queen Victoria's court by wearing shoes and boots made *à la Russe*—i.e., the lefts and rights identical and interchangeable.

Fashion is a form of ugliness so intolerable that we have to alter it every six months.

OSCAR WILDE

Because King Edward VII's consort, Queen Alexandra, had a small scar on her lovely neck and wore a pearl choker to hide it, these "dog collars" became the rage with fashionable London ladies. They also adopted a slight limp, in imitation of hers.

Louis Waller told me that in his opinion it took eight months of continuous wearing to break in a dress coat.

W. PETT RIDGE, *A Story Teller*

"Then," said Madame du Q., "he gave me a sort of chain of sharks' teeth; the kind of thing of which, when it was given to someone at Honolulu, the recipient inquired, '*C'est un collier?*' '*Mais pardon*,' said the donor. '*C'est une robe*'."

AUGUSTUS J. C. HARE, *The Story of My Life*

Anybody wearing anything bearing commercial initials is definitely non-U [i.e., non-upper-class].

BARBARA TUCHMAN, *New York Times*, November 2, 1940

Spats, originally spatterdashes, were also known as galligaskins and antigropelos.

The average person who wears a bow tie is distrusted by almost everyone.

JOHN MOLLOY, a clothing consultant, in *Success*

Molloy also notes that lawyers generally try to keep bow tie wearers off juries, and that men who want to appear trustworthy should stick to their club tie, their diagonal striped tie, or their silk foulard tie.

On neckties with diagonal stripes, the stripes almost always run from the right shoulder down toward the left hip, making the tie of the Alibi Club, in Washington, D.C., unique. As designed by one of its members, Adm. Jerauld Wright, USN, the stripes run from the left shoulder downward to the right. Admiral Wright also designed the club's suspenders and garters: the left one (or side) red (for port), the right green (for starboard).

Crime

As they were going to Execution, the Ordinary asked [Thomas] Reaves [a convicted footpad] if his wife had been concerned with him in any robberies. "No," said he; "she is a worthy woman, whose first husband happening to be hanged, I married her, that she might not reproach me by a repetition of his virtues."

Newgate Calendar

Few men are all bad; and Wainewright, the poisoner, had a pretty taste in art and letters, and Charles Peace, the murderer, played the violin with no ordinary skill.

E. BERESFORD CHANCELLOR,
The Lives of the Rakes

The general public knows that the new invention, the transatlantic wireless telegraph, helped bring about the arrest of Dr. Hawley Harvey Crippen in 1911, when he and his paramour, Ethel Le Neve, fled from London to Canada after he had dismembered his wife; but it is less well known that both the murderer and his victim were American-born. Her maiden name was Kunigunde Mackamotski, but she preferred to call herself Belle Elmore, for which one may hardly blame her.

It is a curious thing about the poisoner: one success almost always makes him try again. The crime for which a poisoner is arrested is usually not his first, nor even his second. The employment of poison gives a sense of power; a feeling which seems to make the poisoner say to himself:

"Nobody knows what a weapon I have. People, if they recognize my power, would respect me more—and fear me more."

Poison is, therefore, frequently the weapon of quiet, furtive people, of small, inoffensive-appearing persons, of meek-looking women; of men who are a little effiminate, a bit sly in manner.

EDMUND PEARSON, *Masterpieces of Murder*

Poison would seem to be the small man's weapon—not only, perhaps, because small men are not given to violence, but also because they often suffer from a sense of inferiority. The remote and generally prolonged action of poison gives them a feeling of power. They can sit back, like gods, and watch it at work.

DOUGLAS G. BROWNE AND E. V. TULLETT,
Bernard Spilsbury, His Life and Cases

. . . that exterminating murder by which, during the winter of 1811–12, John Williams, in one hour, smote two houses with emptiness . . . and asserted his own supremacy above all the children of Cain. . . . He died by his own hand; and . . . was buried in the centre of a *quadrivium*, or conflux of four roads . . . with a stake driven through his heart. And over him drives forever the uproar of unresting London!

THOMAS DE QUINCEY,
"Murder Considered as One of the Fine Arts"

Lizzie Borden took an ax
And gave her mother forty whacks—

What is wrong about this famous couplet? Answer: It wasn't her mother, but her stepmother. (How old do you picture Lizzie at the time of the murder? Forty-five? Fifty? She was thirty-two.)

That most of the homicides of history have been hairy-faced folk, sealed of the tribe of Esau—Cain was certainly unshaven—admits of no dispute.

WILLIAM ROUGHEAD,
Poison in the Pantry, or Dr. Pritchard Revisited

A manual for murderers would contain two strongly worded sections on the dangers of being too greedy, and of antagonizing the victim's relatives and friends. Again and again well-laid schemes have gone wrong through neglect of one or both of these elementary principles.... [Frederick Henry] Seddon gave a pauper's burial to the woman [Eliza Mary Barrow], whose murder brought him several thousand pounds, and took a commission of 12 s. 6 d, from the undertaker.

IB.

[London, 1924. Patrick Mahon was on trial for the murder of Emily Kaye. At Brixton Prison, he had told his defense attorney, J. D. Cassels,] how he built up a great fire in the bungalow [the murder scene], and in it placed Emily Kaye's severed head. The day was stormy, and as the long fair hair flamed up the dead eyes opened, and, at the same instant, thunder crashed overhead and lightning blazed. Terrified, Mahon ran out into the rain. Now, on the third day of the trial, Cassels was again questioning him about those fearful hours when he was cutting and sawing and boiling the remains of the woman who had loved him. The July weather was dark and sultry, and as Cassels began to ask about the head, and Mahon replied, again a thunderclap reverberated through the courtroom, and the lightning flashed. Mahon shrank back, gripping the edge of the witness-box. He was white and shaken....

IB.

[Sir Bentley] Purchase [a London coroner] was putting questions to a landlord whose tenant had gassed himself. His last question was whether the tenant had ever given any indication that he might take his own life.

"It was the last thing I thought he would do," was the emphatic reply.

"Well," said Purchase, "it was, too, wasn't it?"

ROBERT JACKSON,
Coroner, the Biography of Sir Bentley Purchase

Purchase [see above] and [his fellow coroner] Spilsbury [see above] finally devised a formula to break a murderer's neck without stretching it: "Take the weight in pounds, divide into a thousand, and the answer is the foot drop. If the

fellow is more than six feet tall or stoutly built, you add a bit more for safety's sake."

IB.

Mr. and Mrs. Manning murdered a man for his money. . . . Mrs. Manning had been maid to the Duchess of Sutherland, who thought highly of her, and when she was condemned the Duchess wrote to the governor of the prison, asking him if Mrs. Manning might be hanged in a black satin dress and black silk stockings. Black satin went out of fashion after this event for many years.

(MRS.) E. M. WARD, *Memories of 90 Years*

The men who pawned [the murdered man's watch] were traced and taken: Cain and Rain were their odd names. In the hand of the murdered man was found a button of pink glass, imitation amethyst, which exactly matched those on Cain's waistcoat, with a bit of the stuff hanging to it, as if the dead man's hand had clenched it in a struggle. But Cain's friends got hold of the discovery, and sowed the wood with similar pink buttons, which were found; so *that* evidence went for nothing, and Cain got off.

AUGUSTUS J. C. HARE, *The Story of My Life*

Lord Waterford pursued a robber who had broken into his house, finding him in a public-house some four miles off, and convicting him amongst a number of other men by insisting upon feeling all their hearts; the man whose heart was still beating quickly was the one who had just done running.

IB.

The majority of murderers are very incorrect characters.

THOMAS DE QUINCEY,
"Murder Considered as One of the Fine Arts"

If once a man indulges himself in murder, very soon he comes to think little of robbing, and from robbing he comes next to drinking and Sabbath-breaking, and from that to incivility and procrastination. . . . Many a man dates his ruin from some murder or other that perhaps he thought little of at the time.

IB.

When John Reginald Halliday Christie was arrested in 1952 for strangling his wife and at least five other women, and hiding their bodies behind the wallpaper of his house at 10 Rillington Place, London, Eric Ambler suggested that the name of the street be changed to Corpus Christie Lane. It *was* changed, but not to that.

There was no law against parricide in ancient Rome, such a crime not being supposed possible. About 500 years after Numa's reign [about 200 B.C.], L. Ostius having killed his father, the Romans first scourged the parricide; then sewed him up in a leathern sack made air-tight, with a live dog, a cock, a viper, and an ape, and thus cast him into the sea. The old Egyptians used to run sharp reeds into every part of the bodies of parricides; and after having thus wounded them, threw them upon a heap of thorns and set fire to it.

JOSEPH HAYDN, *Dictionary of Dates*

The Cruel Critics

Alexander Woollcott, of a play starring Odette Myrtil: "Odette, where is thy sting?"

Anthony Hope, at a performance of *Peter Pan*: "Oh, for an hour of Herod!"

George S. Kaufman: "I saw the play under the worst possible conditions: the curtain was up."

Robert Benchley: "It was one of those plays in which all the actors unfortunately enunciated very clearly."

Eugene Field, on a certain actor's performance as King Lear: "He played the King as though under momentary apprehension that someone else was about to play the ace."

Oscar Wilde: "The first rule for a young playwright to follow is not to write like Henry Arthur Jones. The second and third rules are the same."

John Mason Brown: "Tallulah Bankhead barged down the Nile last night as Cleopatra—and sank."

Heywood Broun's review of a certain actor's performance said that it was the worst he had ever seen on any stage. The actor sued but lost. When he appeared in another play the following season, the whole fraternity of critics waited to see how Broun would handle the delicate situation. He handled it perfectly, they all agreed. His review said "Mr.——'s performance was not up to his usual standard."

Max Beerbohm, of Sarah Bernhardt as Hamlet: "The only compliment that one can conscientiously pay her is that her Hamlet was *très grande dame*."

Wolcott Gibbs, of a musical comedy called *WHAM!*: "Ouch!"

George Jean Nathan: "Mr.—— writes his plays for the ages—the ages between five and twelve."

At the Pavilion and at the Oxford, I often found myself in sympathy with the gallery man who, at a pause in some dreary entertainment, wailed out, "Oh, my poor shillin'!"

W. PETT RIDGE, *A Story Teller*

Joseph Regan [was] an actor whose performance on any given night might have been presented as an appropriate gift to two people celebrating their wooden anniversary.

MOSS HART, *Act One*

The covers of this book are too far apart.

AMBROSE BIERCE

A Boston reporter took a look at [J.M.W. Turner's painting] "Slave Ship," floundering about in that fierce conflagration of reds and yellows, and said it reminded him of a tortoise-shell cat having a fit in a platter of tomatoes.

MARK TWAIN, *A Tramp Abroad*

Deaths, Strange and Violent

Aeschylus suffered a fatal fracture of the skull in 456 B.C., when an eagle presumably mistook his bald head for a rock and, presumably in order to break the shell of the tortoise it was carrying, dropped it on him.

Louis Joseph Vance, the author of the best-selling *Lone Wolf* stories (about a gentleman crook), died apparently of spontaneous combustion while sitting quietly in his New York apartment in 1933. The press reported that his head and upper torso "looked as if they had been pushed into a blazing furnace," yet his lower torso was hardly burned at all; nor was anything else in the room burned but his chair, which was totally consumed except for the frame.

Isadora Duncan, the dancer, was riding in an open car in Nice in 1927 when her long scarf became entangled in the rear axle, breaking her neck.

Queen Mary's paternal grandmother, Countess Claudia Rhèdey, was on horseback, watching a military review near Vienna in 1841, when her mount bolted and threw her, and a squadron of cavalry galloping past trampled her to death.

The pupils of St. Cassian, a third-century schoolmaster, stabbed him to death with their pens.

Both Leopold I of the Holy Roman Empire (1640–1705) and Pope Clement VII (c. 1475–1534) are said to have died

from inhaling the smoke of candles which had been impregnated with arsenic.

One night in A.D. 762, Li Po, the great Chinese poet, saw the moon's reflection in a placid pond and leaned from his boat to kiss it, but being drunk, fell overboard and was drowned.

Count Hans Axel Fersen (1755–1810) of Sweden, suspected of having poisoned the heir to the throne, was attacked by a mob in Stockholm and beaten to death with umbrellas.

Jean Baptiste Lully (1632–87), the Italian-born French composer, died as the result of what *Baker's Biographical Dictionary of Musicians* calls "a symbolic accident." While conducting, he vehemently struck his foot with a sharp-pointed cane used to pound out the beat; gangrene set in, and he died of blood poisoning.

[Jael] put her hand to the nail, and her right hand to the workmen's hammer; and with the hammer she smote Sisera, she smote off his head, when she had pierced and stricken through his temples.

Judges 5:26

Duke Charles of Lorraine (1643–90) died from wearing a wig which one of his servants had been bribed to steep in poison.

Distinctions

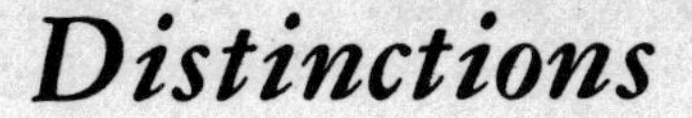

Boat-ship. A *ship* can carry a *boat*, but not vice versa.

Flotsam, jetsam and *lagan*. *Flotsam* is anything floating or drifting about; *jetsam* is goods cast overboard (jettisoned) to lighten a vessel in distress; *lagan* is goods sunk in the sea with a buoy attached, to facilitate recovery.

The blueberry differs from the huckleberry in containing numerous minute seeds instead of ten nutlets.

WEBSTER

There is a popular measure of proportion, with approximate percentages as follows:

(100%) Mr. Jordan's fortune consisted wholly of bar-gold.
(99%) Practically all his fortune consisted of bar-gold.
(95%) His fortune consisted almost entirely of bar-gold.
(80%) By far the greater part of his fortune consisted of bar-gold.
(70%) The greater part of his fortune consisted of bar-gold.
(60%) More than half his fortune consisted of bar-gold.
(55%) Rather more than half his fortune consisted of bar-gold.
(50%) Half his fortune consisted of bar-gold.
(45%) Nearly half his fortune consisted of bar-gold.
(40%) A large part of his fortune consisted of bar-gold.

(35%) Quite a large part of his fortune consisted of bar-gold.
(30%) A considerable part of his fortune consisted of bar-gold.
(25%) Part of his fortune consisted of bar-gold.
(15%) A small part of his fortune consisted of bar-gold.
(10%) Not much of his fortune consisted of bar-gold.
(5%) A very small part of his fortune consisted of bar-gold.
(1%) An inconsiderable part of his fortune consisted of bar-gold.
(0%) None of his fortune consisted of bar-gold.

ROBERT GRAVES AND ALAN HODGE,
The Reader over Your Shoulder

A *stadium* is either oval or circular; an *amphitheater* is elliptical.

A *cenotaph* is a monument to a person or to persons buried elsewhere.

Fort and fortress. A fortress is larger and may comprise a number of forts.

Drinking

One drink is just right; two is too many; three are too few.

Spanish maxim

The first drink with water, the second without water, the third like water.

IB.

He approached the making of a martini as some medieval illuminator approached the compilation of a Book of Hours, or a Japanese noblewoman the tea ceremony.

Anon.

A good Martini should be strong enough to make your eyeballs bubble, and so cold your teeth will ache, and you'll think you're hearing sleigh bells.

L. G. SHREVE

In 1907 Chile had the largest per capita consumption of champagne in the world.

ANDRÉ SIMON

The dew was falling fast, the stars began to blink:
I heard a voice; it said, "Drink, pretty creature, drink!"

WORDSWORTH, "The Pet Lamb"

If all be true that I do think,
There are five reasons we should drink:

Good wine—a friend—or being dry—
Or lest we should be by and by—
Or any other reason why.

HENRY ALDRICH,
"Reasons for Drinking"

I am more afraid of King Alcohol than of all the bullets of the enemy.

STONEWALL JACKSON

I "laced" the cocktails with Benzedrine, which I find always makes a party go.

Chips: The Diaries of Sir Henry Channon

If ever I marry a wife,
I'll marry a landlord's daughter,
For then I may sit in the bar,
And drink cold brandy and water.

CHARLES LAMB

The rapturous, wild, and ineffable pleasure
Of drinking at somebody else's expense.

HENRY SAMBROOKE LEIGH,
"Stanzas to an Intoxicated Fly"

Three recipes for the martini:
[The classic:] "3.7 parts 95-proof gin to 1 part dry vermouth."

BERNARD DEVOTO

(But I have never been able to find 95-proof gin.)

[The Benchley special:] "Gin, and just enough vermouth to take away that nasty, watery look."

ROBERT BENCHLEY

[The matador:] "Vermouth to cover the bottom of a frozen glass, ¾ ounces of gin, and a Spanish cocktail onion."

ERNEST HEMINGWAY

One of the Dukes of Cleveland had his wineglasses made without a foot, so that they would not stand and had to be emptied at a gulp.

I always was ambitious of sitting out every man at the table where I presided; which . . . I generally accomplished, eating sparingly of some one plain dish, avoiding malt liquor and desiring the servants to take away my glass after a hob-nob [i.e., drink] the moment I put it down. . . . When, as was sometimes the case, I felt the wine disposed to revolt, chewing two or three French olives without swallowing the pulp would . . . enable me to get down half a dozen more glasses. By these little fair manoeuvers I established the character of being a capital host.

The Prodigal Rake: Memoirs of William Hickey, edited by Peter Quennell

Baron James Rothschild sent Rossini [composer of *The Barber of Seville, William Tell*, etc.] some splendid grapes from his hothouse. Rossini, in thanking him, wrote, "Although your grapes are superb, I don't like my wine in capsules." Rothschild read this as an invitation to send him some of his celebrated Château-Lafitte, which he proceeded to do.

LILLIE DE HEGERMANN-LINDENCRONE, *In the Courts of Memory*

When the wine [made at her château] is in the golden period of effervescing, any sick child in the village ticketed by the doctor can be brought to the wine-presses and dipped in. If labeled "*très malade*," he is dipped in twice.

IB.

Sometimes a man will tell his bartender things he wouldn't tell his doctor.

Sky Trek

James Branch Cabell used to serve a cocktail called "Ravished Virgin." I don't know what its ingredients were, and I was too shy to ask.

Theologically deeply learned, [the first Earl of] Manchester [1563–1642] published a Protestant treatise which he called *Contemplationes Mortis et Immortalitatis*, in dignified and persuasive prose. It first appeared in 1631, running into fifteen editions by 1688. Hand in hand with piety, he was drunk with every meal.

BRIAN MASTERS, *The Dukes*

Fill your empty glass,
Empty your full glass.
I can't abide in your hand
A glass either empty or full.

RABELAIS

What was silver in the pocket
Becomes gold in the bottle.
What was gold in the bottle
Becomes copper on the nose.
German verse

An expert once told me that excessive drinking of beer is likely to make the consumer fall forward; anyone overestimating his powers in regard to cider invariably falls backward.

W. PETT RIDGE, *A Story Teller*

The custom of saluting [i.e., embracing] ladies by their relatives and friends was introduced, it is said, by the early Romans, not out of respect originally, but to find by their breath whether they had been drinking wine, this being criminal for women to do, as it sometimes led to adultery.

JOSEPH HAYDN, *Dictionary of Dates*

I can't drink as much as I used to, and what's more, I never could.

I. H. C.

[The mad King Ludwig of Bavaria] hardly ever touched any wine but light hock or champagne freely mixed with water, in which violet flowers had been scattered.

HILDEGARDE EBENTHAL, *The Tragedy of a Throne*

Who hath woe? who hath sorrow? who hath contentions? who hath babbling? who hath wounds without cause? who hath redness of eyes?

They that tarry long at the wine; they that go to seek mixed wine.

Proverbs 23:29–30

When the Martini beckons,
No seconds.

JOHN STEINBECK

The wine with the happiest name is the Italian Sorriso di Bacco—"Bacchus's Smile"; and the happiest-named confection is the airy little meringue that the French call *pet de nonne*—"nun's fart."

Lord Palmerston, in his eighties, took to drinking port wine with his breakfast and expressed surprise that he had lived so long without discovering how good it was at that time.

Men with short necks got no business drinking neat whiskey. It don't have time to cool. It hits their stomachs red hot and burns 'em right out.

WALLER MORTON

If you are doubtful of a Brandy, pour a small amount into a glass and add perhaps half a tumbler of boiling water. Then note the color and smell. If the color is clear and the smell clean and spirituous there is nothing wrong. The same test is a good one to apply to whiskey and particularly gin.

JULIAN STREET, *Wines*

The British believe in decanting, and most gourmets of my acquaintance think they overdo it. There is a club in London where even Champagne is decanted.

IB.

In the very name "Burgundy" you can hear barrels being rolled to the cellar, and you can see the ruddy faces of Rembrandt's *bourgeoisie*.

SANCHE DE GRAMONT

Hong Kong is fourth in world consumption of cognac, after the United States, Great Britain and West Germany, but first in per capita consumption.

Bureau National du Cognac

According to Brillat-Savarin, General Bisson, a hero of the Napoleonic Wars, drank eight bottles of wine every day at breakfast.

Pure water is the best of drinks
That man to man can bring,
But who am I, that I should have
The best of everything?

Let princes revel at the pump,
Let peers with ponds make free;
For whiskey, wine or even beer
Is good enough for me.

Anon.

The barman recommended a "lightning whizzer," an invention of his own. He said it was what rabbits trained on when they were matched against grizzly bears, and there was only one instance on record of the bear having lasted three rounds.

P. G. WODEHOUSE, "Extricating Young Gussie"

James Whitcomb Riley was standing near a curb directly in front of a saloon when he enquired of a passing policeman, "Can you tell me the nearest place where a man could buy himself a drink?" The policeman replied, "Why, you're right in front of a saloon now." Riley asked, "Are you sure it's the nearest?"

FRED C. KELLEY, *The Life and Times of Kin Hubbard*

Peter the Great drank hot brandy with pepper in it.

He made the sort of martini which fairly whistles through the rigging.

LAWRENCE DURRELL, "Something à la Carte?"

When Russell Baker was offered a fashionable glass of white wine at a cocktail party, he told his host, "I need the quick blow to the back of the neck: give me a martini."

New York Times, April 22, 1984

Lord Saye and Sele . . . had a very strong constitution, and would drink absinthe and curaçao in quantities which were perfectly awful to behold. . . . [He once instructed a new valet,] "Put two bottles of sherry by my bed-side, and call me the day after to-morrow."

The Reminiscences and Recollections of Captain Gronow

When the Countess of Berkeley, who was the daughter of a butcher of Gloucester, was near eighty years old, I remember one day she had her glass filled with claret till the liquid appeared to form a rim above the vessel that contained it, and, raising it steadily to her lips, looked round the table where sat all her children except Lord Fitzhardinge, and saying, "God bless you all," she drank off the contents without spilling a drop, and, replacing the glass on the table said, "Not one of my sons could do that."

FANNY KEMBLE, *Records of a Later Life*

Mr. [Nathaniel] Hawthorne said, "Why has the good old custom of coming together to get drunk gone out? Think of the delight of drinking in pleasant company and then lying down to sleep a deep strong sleep."

MRS. JAMES T. FIELDS, *Memoirs of a Hostess*

On a wet Sunday the shortest way out of Manchester is through a bottle of Gordon's gin.

English adage

When you have to squeeze a lemon at the dinner table—over smoked salmon, say—you should always use your left hand; otherwise, the acid smell of the lemon will cling to your drinking hand and to the stem of your wineglass.

An English gourmet

I never trust a fighting man who doesn't smoke or drink.

ADM. WILLIAM F. HALSEY

Lord Goddard invited a new member of Pratt's Club to a glass of port. "Thank you, sir. I'd like a small one." Lord Goddard said, "Never have a small glass, my boy. It just goes wambling around looking for damage to do. Have a large glass. It settles down and does you good."

CHARLES GRAVES, *Leather Armchairs*

. . . a description of a rum punch-bowl of the West Indies in the spacious days of the eighteenth century:

"A marble basin, built in the middle of the garden especially for the occasion, served as the bowl. Into it were poured 1,200 bottles of rum, 1,200 bottles of Málaga wine, and 400 quarts of boiling water. Then 600 pounds of the best cane sugar and 200 powdered nutmegs were added. The juice of 2,600 lemons was squeezed into the liquor. Onto the surface was launched a handsome mahogany boat piloted by a boy of twelve, who rowed about a few moments, then coasted to the side and began to serve the assembled company of 600, which gradually drank up the ocean upon which he floated."

Quoted in *Alexis Lichine's Encyclopedia of Wines and Spirits*

On one occasion [Theodore Hook] questioned a bill for ten brandies preferred [*sic*] by an Atheneum Club waiter, claiming that he had taken only nine, and was forthwith reminded of the one that he had enjoyed before he sat down. On another occasion he spent the whole afternoon with an American *bon vivant*, drinking experimental gin and maraschino cocktails by the *pint*—and then dined, calm and sober, at Lord Canterbury's, where he ascribed his poor appetite to "a biscuit and a glass of sherry rashly taken at luncheon."

A. J. A. SYMONS, *Essays and Biographies*

Come quickly! I am tasting stars!

DOM PERIGNON (1638–1714),
at his first taste of champagne

Alcohol is the anaesthesia by which we endure the operation of life.

GEORGE BERNARD SHAW

The population of Krasnensk, a town in Byelorussia, totals only 6,000, yet they consume some 150,000 bottles of vodka *per month*, an average of 25 bottles per month per mouth, including children and infants.

Sunday Times of London

Hangover: a self-inflicted wound.

ANON.

Eating

Lord Lonsdale's breakfast was rather different to the rest of us. He would heap his plate, seat himself at the head of the table and feed each of his dogs in turn from his plate. He himself ate practically nothing. When this performance was over he would light a cigar and drink, at one gulp, a claret glass of brandy. He would follow this immediately with half a bottle of white wine, and then bid everyone a bright good morning, explaining that he must deal with his correspondence.

DOUGLAS SUTHERLAND, *The Yellow Earl*

There are vintage years in sardines, as well as in wines: Oscar Wilde's son Vyvyan Holland founded a vintage sardine club before the last war whose members owned sardine cellars and held reverential tastings. Members decided that the great years for sardines coincided with the years immediately following the great years for Sauternes. Vyvyan Holland counsels 1959 as the best post-war sardine vintage.

Sunday Times [London] *Magazine*

Duncan Gillis, the U.S. runner-up to the hammer-throwing champion in the 1912 Olympic Games, used to eat a dozen raw eggs for breakfast, shells and all, with a dab of mustard on the shells.

Sir Philip Sassoon likened Lobster Newburg to a "purée of white kid gloves."

Chips: The Diaries of Sir Henry Channon

My grandfather had even more violent antipathies toward certain foods. Vanilla ice cream was "chalk and water"; bananas, "wet buckskin dipped in sugar"; and wild duck, "a cigar box wrapped in greasy brown paper."

King George I of England was extremely fond of oysters, but would not eat them until they had begun to spoil.

He had a Way of turning Things over with his Fork, as if to say, "Well, I don't know about this."

GEORGE ADE

The wealthy 18th-century gourmet Grimod de la Reynière said with relief after the [French] Revolution was over, "If it had lasted any longer, we might have lost the recipe for fricassee of chicken."

Quoted by SANCHE DE GRAMONT

How fitting for Brillat-Savarin, the great French gastronomist and author of *The Physiology of Taste*, to have been born in the town of Belley!

Truly fastidious gourmets won't eat soft-boiled eggs with a spoon made of anything but bone or ivory. Silver, they declare, gives an unpleasant taste.

Julius Caesar was once a guest at a dinner in Milan when the asparagus was served doused with perfume instead of olive oil. Seeing that his staff could not get it down, Caesar reproved them for their bad manners and ate the course without comment.

The heart of a French king is preserved at Nuneham in a silver casket. Dr. Buckland, whilst looking at it, exclaimed, "I have eaten many strange things, but have never eaten the heart of a king before," and, before anyone could hinder him, he had gobbled it up, and the precious relic was lost forever. Dr. Buckland used to say that he had eaten his way straight through the whole animal creation, and that the worst thing was a mole—that was utterly horrible. (He afterwards told Lady Lundhurst that there was one thing even worse than a mole, and that was a bluebottle fly.)

AUGUSTUS J. C. HARE, *The Story of My Life*

When the Maharajah of Johore goes out to luncheon or dinner, he sends on his own cook to prepare for him, taking with him, to kill on the spot, the chicken which his master is to eat. When the cook kills it, he says a sort of little prayer —"Dear little brother, forgive me for the pain I am going to inflict upon you; it will only be momentary, and it really cannot be helped."

IB.

King George III's favorite dinner was boiled mutton with turnips. Whenever Queen Charlotte notified him that it was being served, he would run to his harp and strum a gay little tune.

Peasants in Carpathia like to eat raw wolf meat marinated in raw liquor. They also enjoy sandwiches made with American toothpaste.

Such eating and drinking I never saw [as in Jamaica]! I observed some of our party today eat at breakfast as if they had never eaten before. A dish of tea, another of coffee, a bumper of claret, another large one of hocknegus; then Madeira, sangaree, hot and cold meats, stews and pies, hot and cold fish pickled and plain, peppers, ginger-sweetmeats, acid fruit, sweet jellies. . . .

Lady Nugent's Diary, 1801

One ostrich egg will make an omelet large enough to serve six people.

Lord Hastings was accustomed to start the day with a breakfast of mackerel bones cooked in gin.

DOUGLAS SUTHERLAND, *The Yellow Earl*

[Prince Albert, the Prince Consort:] "Things always taste so much better in small houses."

GEORGE W. E. RUSSELL, *An Onlooker's Note-Book*

A lot of chefs stick a banana up a duck and call themselves geniuses.

SANCHE DE GRAMONT,
"French Cooking à la Courtine"

Stilton cheese is always to be sliced, never scooped.... Argument at dinner over whether you are a slicer or a scooper is still considered an excellent choice of topics by some aristocrats.

SIMON WINCHESTER, *Their Noble Lordships*

Cf. the Big-endian vs. Little-endian schism in Lilliput and the division of julep drinkers into opposing and argumentative camps of those who steep their mint and those who muddle it.

The average Mongolian eats more than 500 pounds of meat a year.

Gastronomical perfection can be reached in three combinations: one person dining alone, usually upon a couch or a hillside; two people, of no matter what sex or age, dining in a good restaurant; six people, of no matter what sex or age, dining in a good home.

M. F. K. FISHER

When Salvador Dali was offered his first raw oyster, he shuddered and remarked, "I'd as soon eat a piece of Mae West!"

I saw this item on the menu of a restaurant in Korçë, Albania, in 1927: "Manure . . . 0,05." None of us dared find out what it actually was.

Verdict of a member of the Jury of Testers on a new sauce, as reported by the *Almanach des Gourmands*: "With this sauce a man might eat his father."

LEIGH HUNT, "A Fetching Relish"

I say as Epicurus said, that a man should not so much consider what he eateth as with whom he eateth.

MONTAIGNE, *Essays*

The secret of a successful restaurant is sharp knives.

GEORGE ORWELL

No heresy could be more fatal than the error of permitting two white or brown sauces to appear in sequence, or tolerating the use of truffles twice during the same dinner. Only divine favor could extenuate the crime of offering a *sorbet* —the "Roman punch" which preceded canvasbacks, woodcocks, snipes or truffled capons—flavored with rum; Maraschino or bitter almonds were mandatory.

LLOYD R. MORRIS, *Incredible New York*

Vaughelm, a famous Hungarian sportsman, slew wild boars by the hundreds, but ran away from a table upon which there was a roasted pig, or fainted if he was unable to make his escape.

Sir Charles Mendl told me that before roasting a leg of lamb, one must drag it behind one's yacht for twenty-four hours.

MRS. PHILIP BARRY

Eccentrics

Duke Charles II of Brunswick (1804–73) was known as "the Duke of Diamonds" because he wore them in such profusion that he could have been mistaken for an animated chandelier. He had thirty wigs, all made of black silk thread, drank nothing but iced milk, doused himself with strong violet perfume; took a chessboard to the opera, and had all his clothes made twice too large.

Dr. "Jackey" Barrett, of Trinity College, Dublin, was famous as a Hebrew scholar and as an eccentric. As a rule he prefaced everything he said with the words *Do you see me now.*

"Good morning, Doctor Barrett."

"Do you see me now. Good morning, sir."

Aleister Crowley (1875?–1947), the "wickedest man in the world," filed his teeth to points like a cannibal's and once appeared at the fashionable Café Royal in London with an artificial butterfly pinned to the front of his trousers.

England is the paradise of individuality, eccentricity, heresy, anomalies, hobbies and humours.

GEORGE SANTAYANA

According to the fencing master Angelo, the eccentric Mr. Cuzzans, during a severe frost, "went into the coffee room at Bath, dressed in a complete suit of nankeen, ordered a decanter of cold water, which he poured over his head, over his shoulders, and into his shoes. He then called for a cup of coffee, eggs, and spinach, the *Philadelphia Mercury*, two

pipes, half a lemon and a Welsh rabbit." Later, he ordered a bootjack, a pint of vinegar, a paper of pins, and some barley-sugar, ending with instructions that they should "bring me, after I am in bed, a dish of fried millstones, with a warming-pan, cold without sugar...." He then opened his portmanteau, which he had brought under his arm, put on six shirts over his suit...ordered his bed to be sprinkled with sawdust, and took his leave for the night.

T. H. WHITE, *The Scandalmonger*

Brougham said of [William Pitt, first Earl of] Chatham: "The greatest genius is often marked by eccentricity, as if it disdained to move in the vulgar orbit."

In 1935, on Lord Berners's estate in England, where he kept white doves dyed in all colors, he built a tower 141 feet high and put this sign at its entrance:

MEMBERS OF THE PUBLIC
COMMITTING SUICIDE
FROM THIS TOWER DO SO
AT THEIR OWN RISK.

He had a piano installed in his Rolls-Royce, so that when the mood was on him, he could pull up at the roadside and play.

The fifth Duke [of Portland] was all that a duke might be, habitually wearing three suits, one inside the other... constructing vast subterranean palaces on his Welbeck estate and sacking any of the 500 men employed who saluted him, travelling in a heavily curtained coach drawn by six small ponies, and eating—in two halves—a chicken a day.

Punch

...A very old lady, with great traces of beauty and dignity of manner, but she wore the most extraordinary bonnet, very large, and from the fringe hung a pair of scissors, a thimble, and a needle-book. He made a civil speech to her, about being glad to see her looking so well, or something of that kind. In reply she only just looked up and said, "For further information refer to the 25th chapter of the second book of Kings," and took no more notice whatever.

AUGUSTUS J. C. HARE, *The Story of My Life*

...Donna Ursilia Lovatelli, who likes to converse in Sanskrit.

IB.

Monsieur de Saint-Crick, a baron of wealth and good family, would put in an appearance every afternoon at Tortoni's [in Paris] where, seated at a pavement table, he'd order two ices—one strawberry, one vanilla. When they came, he'd take off his shoes, dump the vanilla into the right and the strawberry into the left. If he made the occasional error of confusing the flavors, he'd empty out his shoes, repeat the order and correct the procedure.

CORNELIA OTIS SKINNER,
Elegant Wits and Grand Horizontals

The professor was an unmarried man with three sisters, all of whom were insane at times, and frequently one of them was away from home in an asylum. One day the brother was away, the eldest sister being at home in apparently good health, when another professor came to visit them to whom she wished to be particularly polite. "What will you have for dinner," said she, "today?" "Oh! the best thing you've got," he replied. So when dinner came, she had stewed the family Bible with cabbage for his repast.

MRS. JAMES T. FIELDS, *Memories of a Hostess*

The successive Lord Norths, of Burgholt House, go to bed each October 9 and don't get up again until the following March 22.

HUGH VICKERS AND CAROLINE MCCULLOUGH, *Great Country House Disasters*

Epitaphs

An epitaph is a belated advertisement for a line of goods that has been permanently discontinued.

IRVIN S. COBB

I have only one ambition left: I should like to have a good epitaph.

PRINCE BISMARCK

There is a small grave under the oak trees at Adare Manor, the seat of the Earls of Dunraven, near Limerick, Ireland. The inscription says, "To Vie, my favorite goldfish, brought from France 1884, died much loved and regretted in 1886."

There used to be a little monument in the garden [Hogarth's, at Chiswick] to his favourite bullfinch, with two crossbones of birds, and a heart, carved on the rough stone by his hand: "Alas! poor Dick," is the inscription.

(MRS.) E. M. WARD, *Memories of 90 Years*

[For a successful crapshooter, Alexander Pope's line] "He lisped in numbers, and the numbers came."

For a lady who loved going to parties: "God called her, and she could go."

Epitaph of Wolfgang Philip von und zu Guttenberg, Bailiff of Brandenburg, Commander of Erddtling, Bruchsal and Weissenburg, in the Co-Cathedral of St. John in Valletta, Malta: *Fumus, humus, sumus; et cinis est nostra ultima finis* ("We are smoke and earth, and our final end is ashes"). Another epitaph, nearby, warns, "You who tread on me, you will be trod upon; reflect on that, and pray for me." Alas, so many have trod on his stone already, his name is quite worn away.

The most dramatic stone in the pet cemetery at Asnières, a suburb of Paris, is Barry's, whose monument is the largest there. His epitaph says, "He saved the lives of forty people. He was killed by the forty-first." Barry was a Saint Bernard (the Swiss hospice looms above him on his towering monument), celebrated throughout the Alps for his heroic rescues. One night the border patrol wounded a smuggler trying to sneak across. He managed to escape capture, but before long he fell, faint from loss of blood. There, in the snow, Barry found him and, as Saint Bernards are trained to do, stretched out on him to keep him from freezing. Soon the smuggler regained semi-consciousness. He was pinioned; the patrol had caught him after all! He fumbled for his knife and stabbed upward, desperately. Barry, dying, crept home to the hospice. The patrol was summoned. It had no trouble backtracking his bloody trail.

On the grave of a dog named Clown, in the same cemetery:

> You who so amused us,
> Now you make us weep.

And for a cat, Mitzou, also there:

> *Je n'avais que toi*
> *Tu n'avais que moi.*
> ("I had only you!
> You had only me!")

For a prize fighter: T I M E.

WALTER DE LA MARE

One of the most moving epitaphs I ever read—actually it is an inscription—is in Ixelles cemetery, Brussels, on the tomb of a girl who had been the mistress of Gen. Georges

Boulanger, a former War Minister of France. She died in July 1891; that September, heartbroken, Boulanger made the supreme romantic gesture, one that many, many bereft lovers have threatened, but very, very few have carried through: He shot himself at her tomb. He is buried beside her, and his last, impassioned cry rings out in bronze:

AI-JE BIEN PU VIVRE
2 MOIS ½ SANS TOI!

("How did I live two and a half months without you!") Romeo said nothing more poignant.

This man, inconsiderable, mean, yes, a slave—this man was loved and was lord of another's soul.

BIANOR

Preston Sturges's, for himself:

Now I've laid me down to die
I pray my neighbors not to pry
But much enjoyed as life flew by

Cecil Clay, Lord Chesterfield's counselor, asked to have this on his tombstone: SUM QUOD FUI ("I am what I was").

When I am dead, I hope it may be said:
"His sins were scarlet, but his books were read."

HILAIRE BELLOC

On the tombstone of the Reform Club's famous French chef Alexis Soyer (1809–58), in Kensal Green Cemetery, London:

SOYER TRANQUIL.

Epitaph for Lord Byron's mastiff Boatswain, who went mad and died in 1808:

Near this spot
Are deposited the remains of one
Who possessed beauty without vanity
Strength without insolence
Courage without ferocity
And all the virtues of man without his vices.
This praise, which would be unmeaning flattery
If inscribed over human ashes,
Is but a just tribute to the memory of
Boatswain, a dog.

[Epitaph for Jack King, a gambler:] "Life ain't in holding a good hand, but in playing a pore hand well."

A. H. LEWIS, "Wolfville's First Funeral"

Sir Max Beerbohm's epitaph for George IV's uncrowned Queen Caroline: "Fate wrote her a most tremendous tragedy, and she played it in tights."

Epitaph for a famous Chicago confidence man:

Yellow Kid Weil lies here underground.
Don't rattle your change while walking around!

Extremes

His forehead was so wrinkled, he had to screw his hat on.

CARLETON ALSOP

His feet were so tough, he wore his shoes out from the inside.

She was so big, she could stand flat-footed and piss in the radiator of a Mack truck.

Thomasville, Ga.

The coffee was so strong, we had to rebore the pot; and so hot, we had to butter our tongues.

M. S. A. R.

We played a theatre so deep in the woods, the manager was a bear—he paid us off in honey. The audience threw owl eggs at us, and woodpeckers ate up the straight man's cane. The only paper that reviewed our act was *Field & Stream*.

FRED ALLEN

Frank Wisner, of Laurel, Miss., had a variation on Allen's classic: "Our house was so far in the boondocks, we had to grease the wagon twice before we got to town. First thing we did in the morning was sweep the coon-farts out of the kitchen. We never got our mail when the creek was high."

His ears stuck out so, he looked like a taxicab coming at you with its doors open.

Said of Clark Gable

Alexander I of Russia was so strong that when he went calling, he would twist a copper kopeck and leave it for his unmistakable visiting card.

Senator Herman Talmadge (of Georgia) was so smart he could give a jaybird the first two pecks and beat him to the bug.

Georgia saying

He was so stupid, he couldn't pour slops from a boot, even with directions engraved on the heel.

He was so big, he could go bear hunting with a switch.

We'll hang him so high, the buzzards won't smell him for three days; and so fast, it'll make a sheep's tail look like a bench mark.

GEN. W. OSCAR BRICE, U.S.M.C.

He was as much slower than stock-still as stock-still is slower than greased lightning.

ALLEN R. FOLEY, *What the Old-Timer Said*

Th' worst sensation I know of is gittin' up in th' night an' steppin' on a toy train o' cars.

KIN HUBBARD, *Abe Martin*

A julep so big that he had to take off his Hat in order to crawl through the Mint and get at the Beverage.

GEORGE ADE

Madam, you could not have surprised me more if you had told me the Virgin Mary had borne twins!

MAJ. ROBERT W. HUNTER, C.S.A.

His legs were so skinny, he could have worn umbrella covers for long drawers.

At Stoke Poges, the inn where we stopped was so small, it could have been spelled "in."

MARY ANDERSON, *A Few Memories*

It rained hard enough to fill a wire basket.

Guinea, Va.

A shingled roof so steep, its top would split a drop of rain.

IB.

A boatbuilder so skilled, he could caulk a picket fence to keep the tide out.

IB.

He was so surprised, his eyes stuck out like a dog's balls.

R. K.

That shotgun could kick the soda out of a biscuit.

Goochland County, Va.

He was so skinny, you could actually see through him in a bright light. At the beach, he once drank too much strawberry pop and looked like a tall thermometer.

MIKE ROYKO

Eyes

The eyes of men converse as much as their tongues, with the advantage that the ocular dialect needs no dictionary, but is understood all the world over.

EMERSON, *Conduct of Life: Behavior*

His eyes were as bright and steadfast as altar candles.

JAMES BRANCH CABELL, *Jurgen*

Her eyes were like two teaspoonfuls of the Mediterranean.

MICHAEL ARLEN

Bagehot said of Lord Brougham, because of a look in his eye: "If he were a horse, nobody would buy him."

The fascinating rattlesnake eye of the murderer [John Williams]. . . . His eyes seemed frozen and glazed, as if their light were all converged upon some victim lurking in the far background.

THOMAS DE QUINCEY,
"Murder Considered as One of the Fine Arts"

An irresistible feline luminosity in the eyes.

IB.

John Wilkes's eyes were of different colors. So were Charles Lamb's; he described himself as "odd-eyed."

John Armstrong Chaloner (of "Who's looney now?" fame) insisted that he had changed the color of his eyes from brown to gray, with the help of a ouija board. It told him, he said, " 'Stand by a window facing west, and with a mirror in one hand and your pearl scarfpin in the other, watch the change in your eyes.' It was complete in fifteen minutes."

Il y avait un vieillard d' Auteuil
Qui n'avait qu'une dent et qu'un oeil,
Mais cet oeil solitaire
Etait plein de mystère,
Et cette dent, de fierté et d'orgueil.

GEORGE DU MAURIER

An eye like the cherry in a Manhattan cocktail.

O. HENRY

I could have lighted my pipe at her eyes!

FREDERICK LOCKER-LAMPSON, *My Confidences*

I've met Hitler, and Atatürk [the Turkish dictator] was fifty Hitlers. His eyes were magnetic without being fanatic.... Bluish-gray, with dark rims around the irises.

THE DUCHESS OF WINDSOR

When George II's Queen Caroline lay dying in 1737, her loving husband informed her that her eyes "looked like those of a calf with its throat cut."

In the years of George III's madness, Queen Charlotte was frightened to see that "his eyes looked like black currant jelly."

It is not true that all murderers have blue eyes, but it is true that they have been a noticeable feature in a number of men whose careers were full of danger to people about them.

EDMOND PEARSON, *Masterpieces of Murder*

Our party met with a most hostile reception in one part of Canton, and the crowd were very menacing. Chinamen have invariably chocolate-coloured eyes, so their wooden figures of devils are always painted with light eyes. It so happened that all four in our party had light-coloured eyes, so the *prima facie* evidence of our satanic origin was certainly strong.

LORD FREDERIC HAMILTON,
Here, There and Everywhere

[Sir John Denham's] eye was a kind of light goose-grey, not big; but it had a strange piercingness, not as to shining and glory, but when he conversed with you, he look'd into your very thoughts.

JOHN AUBREY

Ben Jonson had one eye lower then t'other, and bigger, like Clun, the player: perhaps he begott Clun.

IB.

I saw Napoleon at Elba. He had a dusky grey eye—wha
would be called a vicious eye in a horse.

LORD JOHN RUSSEL

For those who believe the old saw that an honest man mus
have a direct gaze, I refer them to a contemporary's repor
that the shiftiest-eyed man he had ever met was Thoma
Jefferson.

GORE VIDA

His eye, once so kindly, could have been grafted on to th
head of a man-eating shark and no questions asked.

P. G. WODEHOUSE, "The Juice of an Orange"

His eyes were like the eyes of a fish not in the best o
health.

IB., *Big Mone*

Roderick Spode was a big chap with a small moustache an
the sort of eye that can open an oyster at sixty paces.

IB., "The Juice of an Orange"

Up to the mid-nineteenth century, many Swiss believed tha
washing the feet weakened the eyes.

Faux Pas

The Countess of Coventry told King George II that the one sight in London she longed to see was a Coronation.

After George III's Coronation, the Deputy Earl Marshal, Lord Effington, admitted to him that it had been badly bungled but promised that the next one would run more smoothly.

Sir Frederick Ponsonby, King George V's Keeper of the Privy Purse, had a long illness. When his convalescence permitted, the king visited his bedside and remarked, "I'd heard you'd grown a beard, but I see you've shaved it off."

"I did indeed," said Ponsonby, oblivious of the king's own beard. "They're such *dirty* things!"

"Hark! I hear a white horse coming!"

From the "Lone Ranger" radio program

Once at Lausanne I wanted an extra pillow for my bed. Various bells round the walls had different legends beneath them instructive of their use. On one was written: "*Sonnez deux fois pour le sommelier*."

Feeling positive that "*sommelier*" was "pillow," I obediently rang twice. A man appeared.

I said: "*Je veux un sommelier*."

Said he: "*Moi, je suis le sommelier*."

Said I: "*Mais je veux un sommelier pour dormir*," at which he seemed amazed, and at last I saw my idiotic mistake. I had gotten thoroughly mixed up! *Oreiller* is "pillow"; *sommeiller* is "to slumber"; and *sommelier* is the "waiter"!

LADY NORAH BENTINCK,
My Wanderings and Memories

[The ex-Kaiser] told me the story of the Englishwoman who asked her neighbour at a [French] dinner-party: "*Êtes-vous un fumier*?" (A *fumier* is not a smoker but a dunghill.)

The Diaries of Sir Robert Bruce-Lockhart

[The Duke of Windsor's] visits with the French troops [early in World War II] "went down well" and helped lay the foundations for a happy relationship. His flaccid grasp of the French language made a memorable contribution to their happiness at a distinguished luncheon where he was the guest of the French Army. He had the tables in an uproar by proclaiming that after the war, France and England should join hands to make "*un paix formidable*." Unfortunately, *paix* meaning "peace" is feminine, whereas its masculine homonym, *pet*, means "a fart."

J. BRYAN, III AND CHARLES J. V. MURPHY
The Windsor Story

A Portuguese gentleman, a friend of mine, was invited to a dinner in London where he met a lady who attracted him strongly. He wanted to ask if she was free to dine with him the following evening, but his English was halting, and he couldn't remember the word for "free." Suddenly it came to him that when a taxi was free in Lisbon, its "flag" said *livre*, and doubtless London taxis used the same system. So he turned to the lady and asked, "Tomorrow evening are you for hire?"

When General MacArthur returned to the Philippines after his retirement, a young lady on the reception committee asked him, "Is this the first time you have been here, General?"

WILLIAM MANCHESTER

King George V loved to hear his favorite stories repeated, and again and again would ask Lord Louis Mountbatten to describe the visit of his sister Crown Princess (later Queen) Louise of Sweden to Uppsala Cathedral. The Archbishop, determined to show off his knowledge of English, approached a chest of drawers in the sacristy with the startling announcement, "I will now open these trousers, and reveal some even more precious treasures to Your Royal Highness."

KENNETH ROSE, *King George V*

Gambling

Ralph Nevill's *Light Come, Light Go* tells how the number 13 once forced itself on his attention at Monte Carlo. His hotel room in Paris had been 13; his berth on the *Train Bleu* was 13; he arrived in Monte Carlo on the thirteenth of the month, and again his hotel room was 13. So he backed 13—and lost his shirt.

Always feminine, fortune is to all appearances essentially wayward and capricious. She requires to be constantly tended, silently expected, and approached with due caution and prudence. Rough and refractory behavior scares her away; irritation at her eccentricities banishes her altogether; whilst levity and ingratitude, when she is in a beneficent mood, soon cause her to escape. Moderation is the only chance of securing her constant presence.

IB.

A banker from one of the Balkan countries played number 32 at Monte Carlo from the casino's opening at 10:00 A.M. until the last spin of the wheel at 2:00 A.M., only to have 32 turn up not once.

The most popular numbers on the roulette wheel are 17 and 29.

Mangue once came up eighteen times running at Monte Carlo, and *pair* twenty times.

The numbers on the wheel add up to 666, the number of the beast in *Revelation* 13:18: "Six hundred threescore and six." There is no Commandment against gambling, and nowhere in the Bible appear the words *gamble*, *bet*, *wager*, *hazard* and *luck*. However, the Roman soldiers "cast lots" for Jesus's coat.

In the 1820s, Colonel Henry Mellish was the talk of London for having staked £40,000 on a single throw of the dice, and lost. In the 1980s (according to the *Washington Post*), a young man arrived at Las Vegas's Horseshoe Club with a suitcase containing $777,000 in cash, which he exchanged for $500 chips—1554 of them. He bet the whole works (almost four times Mellish's stake) on one roll of the dice, won, and left. All he said was: "This damned inflation was just eroding my money. I figured I might as well double it or lose it."

Woolf Joel made a large fortune in South Africa and brought it with him to Monte Carlo, where he began backing red at trente-et-quarante. After it had turned up twelve times running, bringing him another fortune, he decided to show his gratitude for red's cooperation by giving a "Red Dinner" at the Savoy Hotel in London, in a private dining room which he had had completely redecorated for the occasion. The walls and ceiling were painted red, and a red carpet was laid; the waiters were dressed in red (shirts, collars, ties, socks, and gloves); the flowers on the tables were red; only red wine was served, and only red dishes: shrimp and lobster, mousse of ham with braised red cabbage, fresh strawberries. A few months later, Joel's luck ran out abruptly and forever. Again the dominant color was red—blood-red: He was murdered in his office in Johannesburg.

Milnes' father once said to a friend: "Jack, if you ever hear anyone say I am a gambler, contradict it. I never lost a thousand pounds in a night but twice."

T. WEMYSS REID, *Life, Letters, and Friendships of Richard Monckton Milnes, First Lord Houghton*

A song hit of the 1890s was "The Man Who Broke the Bank at Monte Carlo." The casino's purse is far too fat, of course, for anyone to really "break the bank." The phrase means only to exhaust the reserves at one individual roulette table—an event not at all unusual, since they amount to no more than $12,500. Still, when this happened in the old days, the table was dramatically shrouded in a black crepe sheet, and play was suspended until fresh reserves could be brought up from the main coffers.

The most famous Man Who etc.—the original of the song—was an Englishman. His name was Charles Deville Wells, and he played roulette with the deville's own luck. In three days in 1891, using a version of the martingale system, he broke the bank several times. Wells was bold and lucky. He was also crooked. In 1893 an English court found him guilty of obtaining money under false pretenses and sentenced him to eight years' hard labor. If he had been content to market the ingenious musical skipping rope that he had invented, he might have lived out his life in comfort. Certainly he would have stayed out of prison.

Peter Lind Hayes tells me that he has a companion song to "The Man Who. . . ." That is, he has the *title*. As soon as somebody comes up with the words and music, he'll be ready to go. His title is: "When I Was a Blackjack Dealer, and You Were 21."

Las Vegas means "the Meadows." It has also been translated as "Lost Wages."

Las Vegas's suicide rate is one of the highest in the world: 30.1 per 100,000. The rate for the whole United States is 11.7 per 100,000.

A stickman's reminder at the Landmark Casino in Vegas: "Don't forget, folks: The less you bet, the more you lose when you win!"

André Citroën, the manufacturer of the Citroën automobile, won $125,000 at Deauville one evening and gave each of the four housemen at his table a Citroën as a tip.

The two men who brought Deauville to its fashionable peak after the Great War were Eugène Cornuché and François André. Cornuché got his start as a waiter in Paris; André, as a dishwasher and undertaker's assistant in Marseilles. He earned his first stake by betting he could roll a barrel in a straight line, a trick he had learned as the son of a small brewer.

There is no clock to be seen in any casino in all Las Vegas.

Countess Rattazzi (a.k.a. "Princess Brouhaha") was a disreputable great-niece of Napoleon I, thrice married and, like her great-uncle, twice expelled from France. One of her typical exploits occurred when she allowed (or perhaps persuaded) a man to escort her, stark naked, into the casino at Nice and offer to stake her at baccarat. No takers.

The chief of the legendary "Greek Syndicate," Nico Zographos, said this: "The bank plays with cards, the players play with money." Ian Fleming met Zographos at the casino in Le Touquet in 1938 and idolized him to the extent of plotting a short story in which James Bond would work with him. It never got past page 2. However, Fleming studied the casino's security arrangements and devised a plan for circumventing them. Ten to a dozen professionals, he decided, could do the job.

Cora Pearl, a leading *grande cocotte* of the *belle époque*, had an infallibly successful system for roulette: Her current companion was allowed to pay her losses, and she kept her winnings. In all, she went through some £15,000,000. Her real name was Crouch; her father was the composer of "Kathleen Mavourneen."

Adolphe Grillo heads a staff of seven "physiognomists" who follow the gambling season from French casino to casino: Deauville and Le Touquet in summer; Cannes, Nice and Monte Carlo in winter. Two or more of Grillo's men are on duty throughout the play. While you are buying your ticket, one of them is making a lightning sketch of your distinctive features—thick eyebrows, say, snub nose, long earlobes—and adding a few shorthand notes: a red dot for the Legion of Honor, a red line for a known *poule*, "RTM" for "*rousse, taille moyenne*" (redhead, medium figure), a Greek *D* for "doubtful; watch him!," a circle with a tail for a monocle. A blue pencil indicates a man; red, a woman. Sketch and notes together take no more than fifteen seconds. With each physiognomist turning out from 50 to 200 a night, Grillo's file now numbers more than half a million white cards, plus some 10,000 red ones. Red means "barred," though not necessarily by the police or the casinos; some 2,000 poor devils, compulsive gamblers all, have asked Grillo's help in barring themselves.

The best-known "pit boss" at Vegas was the late Sherlock Feldman, who presided over the crap table at the Dunes. One evening a crapshooter became so excited that his upper plate popped out and fell onto the table. Feldman took out his own plate and laid it on the line. "You're faded," he said. (In French casinos the pit boss is the *chef de partie*; in American slang he is the "game warden.")

The Hungarian Count Hunyady [was] the chief gambler of the day [in Paris, after Waterloo]. His luck for a long time was prodigious, and at one time he must have been a winner of nearly two millions of francs. His manners were particularly calm and gentleman-like; he sat apparently unmoved, with his right hand in the breast of his coat, whilst thousands depended upon the turning of a card. His valet, however, confided to some indiscreet friend that his nerves were not of such iron temper as he would have made people believe, and that the count bore in the morning the bloody marks of his nails, which he had pressed into his chest in the agony of an unsuccessful turn of fortune. . . . A run of bad luck set in against him, and he lost not only the whole of the money he had won, but had to borrow £50 to take him back to Hungary.

The Reminiscences and Recollections of Captain Gronow

A Gentleman—

—never wears a new suit: he hangs it out in the rain for two weeks, with stones in its pockets, to give it character.

THE DUKE OF BEDFORD

—never looks as though he had just had a haircut.

—never wears a brown suit or a wool tie.

DOUGLAS FAIRBANKS, JR.

—never is rude unintentionally.

—never asks for a drink; he asks for "something to drink."

AUGUSTUS J. C. HARE to Somerset Maugham,
"The Vagrant Mood"

—is ragged sooner than patched.

DON QUIXOTE

—must have three copies of a book: one for show (and this he will probably keep at his country house), another for use, and a third at the service of his friends.

RICHARD HEBER

—always lifts the seat.

—leaving a nightclub with his girl, always buys *two* copies of the same morning newspaper.

MARLENE DIETRICH

—never strikes a lady with his hat on.

FRED ALLEN

—has never heard a story before.

MARK TWAIN, at a banquet where a speaker said, "If any of you gentlemen have heard this story before, please stop me."

—is often seen, but never heard, to laugh.

LORD CHESTERFIELD

—never looks out of the window [doing so would be an admission of curiosity and lack of self-possession].

ARTHUR MACHEN

—ought not to run or walk too fast in the Streets, lest he be suspected to be going [i.e., delivering] a Message; nor ought his pace to be too slow; nor must he take large Steps, nor too stiff and stately, nor lift his Legs too high, nor stamp hard on the Ground, neither must he swing his Arms backward and forward, nor must he carry his knees too close, nor must he go wagging his Breech, nor with his feet in a straight Line, but with the In-side of his Feet a little out, nor with his Eyes looking down, nor too much elevated, nor looking hither and thither, but with a sedate countenance.

DESMOND MORRIS, *Bodywatching*, quoted from an early eighteenth-century prescription for walking like a gentleman

The man who is always talking about being a gentleman never is one.

R. S. SURTEES, *Ask Mama*

Geography Quiz

(ANSWERS ON NEXT PAGE)

Most Americans know that the Pacific end of the Panama Canal is *east* of the Atlantic end and that Reno is *west* of Los Angeles, but—

1. How many countries does Brazil border?
2. Name at least ten foreign cities beginning with the letter *M* with populations of a million or more.
3. What U.S. state capital is not served by a railroad?
4. Lhasa, Tibet, is south of which of these American cities: Portland (Maine); Boston; New York; Washington; Norfolk; Charleston; Savannah; Jacksonville?
5. What is the relation in longitude between Tahiti and Hawaii?
6. What is the relation in latitude between Venice and Vladivostok?
7. All South America is east of which of these U.S. cities: San Francisco, Denver, St. Louis, Chicago, Cleveland, Pittsburgh, New York?
8. What is the highest point on the east coast of the United States?
9. The great circle route from Tokyo to the Panama Canal enters the U.S. where?
10. If you go due south from Detroit, what is the first foreign country you strike?
11. What is the second-largest French-speaking city?
12. Santa Fe, NM, is our highest state capital, 6950'; what is the next highest?
13. What is the world's largest lake? The world's oldest? The world's deepest?
14. What is "Bimshire"?
15. The largest Greek-speaking city is of course Athens; the second-largest is New York. What is the third?

16. Quick! Is there any of the United States that has a common frontier with only one other state? Quick!
17. The Battle of Trafalgar was fought nearest to which of these ports: Plymouth, Bordeaux, Lisbon, Cádiz, Barcelona, Marseilles, Alexandria?

GEOGRAPHY QUIZ *(Answers)*

1. Ten. They are, counterclockwise, French Guiana, Suriname, Guyana, Venezuela, Colombia, Peru, Bolivia, Paraguay, Argentina, and Uruguay.
2. Madras, Madrid, Manila, Melbourne, Mexico, Milan, Montevideo, Montreal, Moscow, Mukden, Munich.
3. Annapolis.
4. All of them.
5. Tahiti is 500 miles east of Hawaii.
6. Vladivostok is 150 miles south of Venice.
7. The first five.
8. Cadillac Mountain, elevation 1,530 feet, on an island just off the coast of Maine.
9. North Dakota.
10. Canada.
11. Montreal.
12. Cheyenne, WY, 6100'.
13. Lake Baikal, in Siberia, is all three. It is 1.2 miles deep, and of the total volume of water in all the world's lakes, it contains one-sixth.
14. The Barbadians' affectionate name for their island.
15. Melbourne.
16. Maine.
17. Cádiz.

Horses

"The horse of horses," the one that many authorities consider the greatest in all turf history, was foaled during the total eclipse of April 1, 1764, so his name dictated itself. Eclipse was a consistent winner from the start; his owner once watched him lead the field home and made a report that passed into popular usage: "Eclipse first, the rest nowhere." The average racehorse's heart weighs about nine pounds; when Eclipse died, at the age of twenty-five, his was found to weigh fourteen. (The Duke of Wellington's charger, Copenhagen, was a grandson of Eclipse.)

The Aga Khan, of his horse Tulyar, which won the Derby and the St. Leger in 1952: "He was tiny and he had the curious trick of running with his head lower than his withers. Lord Rosebery told me that Eclipse, who was the ancestor of almost all the best thoroughbreds, used to run 'as if he were smelling his way.'"

A colt foaled in May will lie down in running water.

Horsemen's Credo

Carbine could not bear to get his ears wet, and once, when he was being saddled and bridled to run, it began to rain. For some time he refused to go out of his box: so, in desperation, his trainer Higginbotham put up an umbrella, and walked to the starting post carrying this over the horse's head. When he was at the starting post he paid no further attention to the wet, however—and he won the race. In consequence of this idiosyncrasy Higginbotham had a leather protector made like a small umbrella which he attached to the bridle, so that rain could not fall on Carbine's ears.

THE DUKE OF PORTLAND,
Memories of Racing and Hunting

America's premier horseman [in the early nineteenth century], Colonel William Tayloe of Mount Airy, Virginia, once had a mare named Sweetest When Naked.

Skinner's American Turf, vol. i

General Philip Sheridan's horse was named Rienzi, for Wagner's opera.

THE HORSE'S PLEA

Up the hill push me not;
Down the hill rush me not;
On the flat spare me not;
In the stable forget me not.

Anon.

The Kentucky Derby was clocked in quarter-seconds until 1906, when it began being (and still is) clocked in fifths of a second.

Mrs. Payne Whitney, late owner of the Greentree Stable, greatly enjoyed Ernest Hemingway's stories, particularly his "Fifty Grand"—so much so that when a handsome and promising young colt came along, she chose Fifty Grand for his name. It had already been taken, she was told, so she settled for Twenty Grand. He went on the win the Kentucky Derby in 1931 and to become one of Greentree's superstars, but I never heard another word of Fifty Grand.

Argentine gauchos believe that repeated murmurs of "*Pingo! Pingo!*" will soothe the most fractious horse.

Lord Lonsdale would demonstrate the exact control he had over his mount by placing two plates on the ground on the blind side of a jump. He would then put his horse over in such a way that its two *hind* feet landed exactly in the middle of the plates.

DOUGLAS SUTHERLAND, *The Yellow Earl*

In 1904, two fishermen in the Irish Sea saw a horse gravely regarding them from a tiny island. They rescued him and learned that he had been shipwrecked on his way from New Zealand to Liverpool. Moifaa, as he was named, went on to win the world's most trying steeplechase, the Grand National.

Match these famous horses with their owners:

1. Alborak and Fadda	a. Alexander the Great
2. Black Beauty	b. Bellerophon
3. Bucephalus	c. Caligula
4. Xanthus and Balius	d. Barney Google
5. Flicka	e. Squire Gordon
6. Grane	f. Stonewall Jackson
7. Incitatus	g. John Jorrocks
8. Little Sorrell	h. Robert E. Lee

9. Pegasus
10. Rosinante
11. Silver
12. Silver Blaze
13. Sparkplug
14. Tony
15. Traveller
16. Trigger
17. Xerxes and Artaxerxes

i. The Lone Ranger
j. Ken McLaughlin
k. Muhammad
l. Don Quixote
m. Roy Rogers
n. Colonel Ross
o. Siegfried
p. Tom Mix
q. Achilles

1, k. 2, e (*Black Beauty*, by Anna Sewell). 3, a. 4, q. 5, j (*My Friend Flicka*, by Mary O'Hara). 6, o. 7, c (Caligula created Incitatus ["Swift"] a consul). 8, f. 9, b. 10, l. 11, i. 12, n ("Silver Blaze," a Sherlock Holmes story by Sir Arthur Conan Doyle). 13, d. 14, p. 15, h. 16, m. 17, g (*Handley Cross*, by R. S. Surtees).

A separate chapter could be written on the names of race horses—how all of Colonel E. R. Bradley's had names beginning with *B*, like his own (Bimelech, Burgoo King, Broker's Tip, etc.); how all of Lady Beaverbrook's have seven letters (Bustino, Promote, Million, etc.); and how some owners show positive brilliance in choosing a name, as when a mare named The Islander was covered by one of three stallions. Which one? No matter. The witty Lord Knutsford named the colt Trinidad.

Illusions/Delusions

Maupassant appears to be suffering from delusions of grandeur, believing that he has been made a count and insisting that he be addressed as "M. le Comte."

Paris and the Arts, 1851–1896, from the *Goncourt Journal*

Maupassant also believed that he was the son of God, that there were diamonds in his urine, and that a branch planted in the hospital garden would sprout little Maupassants.

Lewis Carroll believed that he saw moving fortifications.

James Harrington, a gentleman of Charles I's bedchamber, "grew to have a phancy that his perspiration turned to flies, and sometimes to bees."

JOHN AUBREY

[George] Cruikshank labored under a strange delusion regarding the works of Dickens. . . . I heard him announce to a large company assembled at dinner at Glasgow that he was the writer of *Oliver Twist*. Dickens, he said, just gave parts of it a little "literary touching up," but he, Cruikshank, supplied all the incidents as well as the illustrations. "Mind, sir," he said to me, "I had nothing to do with the ugly name Dickens would insist on giving the boy. I wanted him called Frank Steadfast."

W. P. FRITH, *My Autobiography and Reminiscences*

Field Marshal Blücher believed that he was pregnant with an elephant, begotten on him by a French soldier.

Lord Northcliffe (1865–1922), the founder of the *London Daily Mail*, died believing that he had been poisoned by German ice cream.

When [Stonewall Jackson] left the U.S. service, he was under the impression that one of his legs was getting shorter than the other. Afterwards his idea was that he only perspired on one side, and that it was necessary to keep the arm and leg of the other side in constant motion in order to preserve the circulation, but it seems that immediately the war broke out, he never made any further allusion to his health.

The Fremantle Diary, edited by Walter Lord

[In] the account of one of the Antarctic expeditions (I think one of Shackleton's) it was related that the party of explorers, at the extremity of their strength, had the constant delusion that there was *one more member* than could actually be counted.

T. S. ELIOT, *Notes on "The Waste Land"*

One of Shelley's neurotic hallucinations was that eyes were staring at him from the breasts of his wife, Mary Godwin.

EDWARD S. GIFFORD, *The Evil Eye*

Evelyn Waugh believed (or professed to believe) that Tito was a woman.

George IV . . . had a singular propensity, in fact a sort of madness, for conceiving that he played a personal part in all the events which had passed in his reign. Amongst other fancies of this sort he believed that he had been on the great battle-field which had terminated the war in 1815; and I have been told by a person present that one day at dinner, after relating his achievements on this occasion, he turned round to the Iron Duke and said:

"Was it not so, Duke?"

"I have often heard Your Majesty say so," replied the Duke drily.

SIR HENRY LYTTON BULWER, *Historical Characters*

Inventions

The street-corner mailbox was invented by Tobias Smollett.

The metal rack to hold a hat under a theater seat was invented by Whittaker Chambers's grandfather.

Life Saver candies were invented by Hart Crane's father.

Roulette was invented by Descartes.

The wheelbarrow is said to have been invented by Blaise Pascal.

Mayonnaise was invented by the Duc de Richelieu.

A system for writing in the dark was invented by Charles Lutwidge Dodgson (Lewis Carroll).

Lobster à la Newberg (*sic*) was invented by Lorenzo Delmonico, of the famous New York restaurant. He called it originally "Lobster à la Wenberg," after a friend, but they quarreled, and he changed its name to Newberg.

The water closet was invented by Sir John Harington, a godson of Queen Elizabeth I. The modern flush toilet was invented by Thomas Crapper of London, "By Appointment to His Majesty George V, Sanitary Engineer."

The "Johnny Mop" was invented by Mrs. Richard Rodgers.

The clyster was invented by the ibis, according to ancient Egyptians.

The game of "cribbage" was invented by Sir John Suckling [1609–42].

JOHN AUBREY, *Lives*

The spherical bowl for goldfish was invented by—rather, sponsored by—Louis XIV's mistress, Madame du Barry.

The Devil himself has at least two inventions to his discredit: the wire coat hanger and the tin wastebasket. Wire coat hangers not only collapse, but are self-tangling; it is impossible to take *one* from a coatrack. As for tin wastebaskets, drop an empty tube of shaving cream or toothpaste into one of them, and it clangs like the gong of an old-fashioned fire engine.

[In 1606, Leo Pronner made a magic knife for an Austrian archduke.] The handle hid 13 drawers containing Psalms written on parchment in 21 languages, and they were attached to 1500 various instruments, 100 pieces of gold and a chain more than 15 cm. long made of 100 gold rings. *The Encyclopaedia of the Plastic Arts* describes this knife as not more than 10 cm. long, but even so it managed to contain a cherry stone on which were heraldic blazons, 24 pewter plates, 12 steel knives, as many wooden spoons and a child's hair split into 12 strands.

MAURICE RHEIMS, *The Strange Life of Objects*

There is an immortal entry in the Minutes of the Paris Academy of Sciences recording the reception of the first phonograph: "No sooner had the machine emitted a few words than the Permanent Secretary threw himself upon [the man conducting the demonstration], seizing his throat in a grip of iron. 'You see, gentlemen,' he exclaimed, 'what it is. . . .' But, to the stupefaction of everyone present, the machine continued to utter sounds."

LOUIS PAUWELS AND JACQUES BERGER,
The Morning of the Magicians

Irritants

Persons who open conversations with "I'll bet you don't remember me."

Drivers ahead who forgetfully leave the left-side blinker on, so that you don't dare pass.

Persons who can't decline a proffered cigarette without adding, "I don't smoke."

Shop clerks who don't wear uniforms or badges to distinguish themselves from customers.

"How ya doin'?" and "Good-bye now!" and "Have a good day!"

Hotel switchboard operators who ring a room for you, and ring and ring, and keep on ringing long after it's obvious there's no one in, and who won't come back on the line so that you can leave a message.

Girls who rechristen themselves "Toni" or "Bettye" or "Jayne" or "Jeri" and such.

Letters that begin "A computer has selected your name" and those that begin "Dear J. Bryan, III."

Service stations that advertise gasoline at "—and *nine-tenths* cents" per gallon.

Personal conversations in elevators.

The whiny voices of children in TV commercials.

Bridge rails at eye level, blocking a motorist's view. Ned Stone maintains that a construction man who wants to specialize in building bridges must first go to a secret graduate school in Utah, where he is taught to design bridge rails that will block the maximum view with the minimum surface and expense. (I have been told that the rails are designed thus on purpose, so that the view won't distract the driver's attention from the road.)

Being put on hold and having a radio at the other end blare into your ear while you wait.

The film shows two persons in the front seat of a car. The driver turns to look at the other, and keeps on looking, and doesn't return his eyes to the road until—if this weren't a "process" shot—the car must inevitably go astray or run into something.

"Xmas" instead of "Christmas."

Gewgaws dangling from the driver's mirror.

Sugar and crackers in paper envelopes.

Guest-room hand towels, new and slick, with all the absorbency of oilcloth.

"We ran into a great friend of yours on our trip. He asked particularly to be remembered to you. Unfortunately I didn't quite catch his name: Dunn, Baldwin, Royster—something like that."

All such vogue words and phrases as: empathy, charisma, simplistic, feedback, input and interface, biodegradable, counterproductive, decorator colors, steel-belted radial, it's a third-down situation, there's a flag on the play, it's a whole new ball game, that's what it's all about, gut feeling, viable, relevant, expertise, hopefully, mind-boggling, state of the art, hypothermia, hairstyling, task force, in depth, thrust, close personal friend, nitty-gritty, bottom line, 'n, the wonderful world of ——, soft underbelly (is there an overbelly, and is it hard?), built-in and locked-in (as "locked-in goodness"), foot-dragging, literally (to add emphasis), drapes (for curtains), foreseeable future, track record, at this point in time, workshop, breakthrough, happenstance, firmly ensconced, fortuitous (for fortunate), if——did not exist, it would have to be invented; ——where anything can happen and probably will; implement (as a verb); fashion-magazine cuteness: "tummy" for stomach, "derrière" for bottom; nice-nellyisms like "full-figured" for buxom; and pretentiousness: *parfum*, *crème*.

Window stickers on new automobiles, listing as "extras" everything but the chassis and body.

Those gabbled and garbled announcements by flight stewardesses, in which you can understand only the dispensables, such as "And I want to take this opportunity to thank you for flying Carpet."

"Wait till I get a pencil."

Having someone you just met call you by your first name.

Round, smooth doorknobs, impossible for a wet hand to turn.

"Salespersons."

The address label pasted across the illustration on the cover of a magazine, and the pharmacist's price label pasted across the instructions on a bottle of medicine.

The interminable lists of credits on TV programs, including such gassy titles as "Production Co-ordinator," "Supervising Editor," and "Project Control Lighting Director."

Languages

If a Portuguese lady should announce that she is *costipada*, don't be dismayed; it means only that she has a bad cold.

The Basques like to say that Adam wooed Eve in Basque and that their language is so difficult, the Devil gave it up after studying it for seven years without learning how to pronounce his own name. (I have heard that a dozen or more Basque words are identical with Japanese, but I have never been able to confirm this.)

"The cock crows *kiao-kiao* in Chinese, and *dchor-dchor* in Mandshu."

MAX MÜLLER, *Lectures on the Science of Languages*

Gabriel taught Joseph seventy languages overnight.

Talmud Sotah, fol. 36

St. Sabinus (ob. 566) understood the language of birds.

Words we need in English:

Magari! (Italian): "Would that it were so!"

cursi (Spanish) or *moche* (French): "tacky"

razliubito (Russian): the feeling you have for someone you once loved, but now no more.

porte-douleurs (French): someone to share your sorrows

gemütlich (German): "cozy, comfortable"

The English language's greatest need is different words for the objective and possessive of the feminine personal pronoun.

ROBERT GRAVES

Prestidigitateur, French for "sleight-of-hand artist," is the most fun to pronounce of any word I know. Next is *bimbibambaka*, Basque for "pealing of bells."

The Hindustani word for *match* is *deussali*, which is said to be a corruption of the cockney soldier's "Gi' us a light." Similarly, in parts of Liechtenstein, the word for a pocket watch is *kelleretli*, a corruption of the French *Quelle heure est-il?*

The Hawaiian alphabet has only twelve letters: A, E, I, O, U, H, K, L, M, N, P, W.

English is the only language egotistic enough to capitalize *I*; German and Spanish courteously capitalize *you* (*Sie*, *Usted*).

In normal speech there are four times as many consonants as vowels, corresponding to the relation between breathing and blood circulation (eighteen breaths to seventy-two pulse-beats).

NOAH JONATHAN JACOBS, *Naming Day in Eden*

Charles V [of Spain] held that Spanish should be spoken to the gods, French to men, Italian to ladies, German to soldiers, English to geese, Hungarian to horses and Bohemian to the devil.

IB.

American is a very difficult language mixed with English.

Anonymous Englishman

[German:] "The grinding gibberish of the garrulous Goth."

SIR RAINALD KNIGHTLEY

Great Britain and the United States are nations separated by a common language.

GEORGE BERNARD SHAW

Dirkovich talked in "purring, spitting Russian."

RUDYARD KIPLING, "The Man Who Was"

George Borrow, the author of *Lavengro* and other books, spoke thirty languages, including Romany, Old Norse, and Manchu. Cardinal Mezzofanti of Bologna was fluent in "some fifty or sixty," according to the *Encyclopaedia Britannica*. M. D. Berlitz, inventor of the Berlitz system for teaching languages, spoke fifty-eight. And his grandson, Charles Berlitz, tells us that Sir John Bowring, once the British Governor of Hong Kong, could speak 100 languages and read 100 more.

Queen Victoria celebrated her seventieth birthday by beginning lessons in Hindustani.

Benjamin Schulze (1699–1760) could recite the Lord's Prayer in 215 languages.

Can you recognize *one word* of the following?

Missierna li inti fis-smewwiet jitquaddes isnek, tigi salnatek, ikun li trid Int, kif fissema hekda fl-art, hobzna ta'kull jum aghtina l-lum, ahfrilma dnubietna, bhalms nahfru lil min hu hati ghalina.

U la ddahhalniex fit-tigrib, izda ehlisna mid-deni Hekk-ikun.

It is the Lord's Prayer in Maltese.

Macaulay once used a Norwegian dictionary to translate the New Testament into Lapp, "thus gaining a superficial knowledge of both languages."

They spoke nothing but Jap, . . . which sounds like someone sandpapering a cheese-wire.

LAWRENCE DURRELL, "White Man's Milk"

General McAuliffe's retort "Nuts!" to a German demand that he surrender was translated by a copy editor on a French newspaper as "You are nothing but old nuts!" And when the heavy in a western movie slammed his fist down on the bar, shouting, "Gimme a shot o' redeye!", the French subtitle read, "*Un Dubonnet, s'il vous plaît.*"

[Classical] Greek had all the merits of other tongues without their accompanying defects. It had the monumental weight and brevity of the Latin, without its rigid unmanageability; the copiousness and flexibility of the German without its heavy commonness and guttural superfluity; the pellucidity of the French without its jejuneness; the force and reality of the English without its structureless comminution.

FREDERIC MYERS, *Essays—Classical*

Russian possesses the vivacity of French, the strength of German, the softness of Italian, the richness and powerful concision of Greek and Latin.

MICHAEL LOMONOSOV

For *seventy, eighty, ninety*, the French say *soixante-dix, quatre-vingts, quatre-vingt-dix*, whereas French-speaking Belgians say *septante, octante, nonante*.

Last Words

King George IV, to his page Sir Walthen Waller: "Wally, what is this? It is death, my boy; they have deceived me!"

H. G. Wells: "Go away! I'm all right."

Lord Chesterfield, to a servant: "Give Dayrolles a chair."

Goethe: "*Mehr Licht!*" ("More light!")

O. O. McIntyre, to his wife: "Turn your face this way, so I can see you."

Archdeacon Julius Hare: "Upwards! Upwards!"

Edmund Gwenn, the actor: "Dying is easy. Comedy is difficult."

Henry Labouchere, M.P. and journalist, when a lamp overturned by his deathbed: "Flames?—not yet, I think."

Sam Bass, a condemned outlaw, an instant before the trap was sprung: "It don't signify."

Oscar Wilde, dying in a bedroom in a French hotel: "Either that wallpaper goes, or I do." (*This is doubtful.*)

Eleonora Duse: "*Agir! Agir!*" ("Do something! Do something!")

Tallulah Bankhead: "Bourbon."

The younger Pitt: "I think I could eat one of Bellamy's pork pies." (There is a theory that what he actually said was "I think I have eaten," etc.)

Gen. John Sedgwick, U.S.A., at the Battle of Spotsylvania Courthouse (1864): "Why, they couldn't hit an elephant at this dist—"

Rabelais: "*Tirez le rideau. La farce est jouée.*" ("Draw the curtain. The farce is over.")

Lady Mary Wortley Montagu. "It has all been very interesting."

William Palmer, the poisoner, as he mounted the scaffold: "Is it safe?"

The deaf Beethoven: "I shall hear in heaven."

O. Henry: "Turn up the light. I don't want to go home in the dark."

King George V, to his family, who were trying to persuade him that he soon would be well enough to revisit his beloved Bognor: "Bugger Bognor!"

George Appell, the Chicago murderer, as he was being strapped in the electric chair: "Well, folks, you are about to see a baked Appell."

Leigh Hunt: "I don't think I shall ever get over this."

Cecil Rhodes: "So little done, so much to do!"

Edith Sitwell, on being asked how she felt: "I am dying, but otherwise quite well."

Sir Walter Raleigh, to the headsman: "Strike, man! Why dost thou not strike?"

King Charles II, referring to his mistress, Nell Gwyn: "Don't let poor Nelly starve!"

Madame de Pompadour, to the curé of the Madeleine, who had called to see her and was now taking his leave "*Un moment, Monsieur le curé, et nous nous en irons ensemble.*" ("One moment, *Monsieur le curé*, and we'll leave together.")

Gainsborough: "We are all going to heaven, and Van Dyck is of the company."

Fontenelle: "*Je ne souffre pas, mes amis, mais je sens une certaine difficulté d'être.*" ("I'm not suffering, my friends, but I feel a certain difficulty in existing.")

[Lord Middlehurst] did not speak again till just before he died, when he kissed his wife's hand with a singular tenderness, and called her Elizabeth. She had been christened Augusta Frederica, but then, as the doctors explained, dying men often make these mistakes.

JOHN OLIVER HOBBES, *The Sinner's Comedy*

Archduke Franz Ferdinand of Austria, mortally wounded by an assassin at Sarajevo on June 28, 1914: "It is nothing."

Stonewall Jackson: "Let us pass over the river, and rest under the shade of the trees."

Brendan Behan, to the nun who was bathing his forehead: "Thank you, Sister! May all your sons be bishops!"

Lord William Russell, having wound his watch: "I have no need of time. I am going to eternity."

John Adams, dying on July 4, 1826, the fiftieth anniversary of the Declaration of Independence: "Thomas Jefferson still survives." But Jefferson had died earlier that same morning, saying, "I resign my soul to God and my daughter to my country."

Chekhov: "It's a long time since I drank champagne."

Gen. Robert E. Lee: "Strike the tent!"

Thomas A. Edison: "It's very beautiful over there."

Citizen Kane: "Rosebud . . ."

Alfred de Musset: "This lovely thing, peace!"

Napoleon: "My son . . . The Army . . . Desais . . ." (Desais was a friend of his youth, killed at Marengo.)

Marcus Aurelius, trying to rise from his deathbed: "An emperor should die standing up!"

Lope de Vega, on being assured that he was indeed dying: "Dante makes me sick!"

Casanova: "Mamma . . . Mamma . . ."

George Washington: "I have long been partial to the river view, Doctor."

Sir Max Beerbohm, to his secretary: "You will find my last words in the blue folder."

The Law

Of Lord Northbury, a hanging judge, it was said that he was only once in his life known to shed tears, and that was at *The Beggar's Opera*, when the reprieve arrives for Captain Macheath.

W. R. LE FANU, *Seventy Years of Irish Life*

Another hanging judge was Lord Braxfield (1722–99), a Scot, whom the *Dictionary of National Biography* (British) describes as "coarse and illiterate, with rough eyebrows, powerful eyes, threatening lips, and a low, growling voice. He was like a formidable blacksmith." He told an eloquent culprit. "Ye're a verra clever chiel, but ye wad be nane the waur o' a hanging." And to a plaintiff who submitted that all great men had been reformers, "even our Saviour himself," Braxfield chuckled. "Muckle he made o' that, my mannie! He was hangit."

Roger B. Taney, chief justice of the Supreme Court from 1836 to 1864, never attended law school.

Lord Campbell, addressing a dinner of the Royal Academy, said that he had difficulty finding anything in common between artists and lawyers, "Unless it is that we lawyers are sometimes said to make coloured representations of the matters we deal with."

HENRY HOLIDAY, *Reminiscences of My Life*

Courting an attorney in order to obtain professional employment is known as huggery and is illegal in England. It is also illegal there to pay a man his wages in a public house, to fire a cannon within 300 yards of a dwelling, to train a boy as a contortionist before he is twelve, or to hypnotize him before he's twenty-one; but it *is* legal for the postmaster-general to refuse letters posted in red envelopes.

In mourning for Queen Anne's death in 1714, judges first donned the black robes they have worn ever since.

Among the useful apophthegms [of Sir Henry Curtis-Bennett, K.C.], was that one should never despair when defending a case which involved indecency. "Six of the jury won't believe that such things happen," he said, "and the other six do it themselves."

SIR RICHARD JACKSON, *Occupied with Crime*

A friend of mine, a member of a certain London club, told me about an evening when the Lord Chief Justice and the Lord Chancellor, the two mightiest powers in the world of English law, also dined there—dined long and liquidly. Afterward, strolling up St. James's Street arm in arm, they began to troll a lusty and somewhat bawdy catch. A young constable on the beat overheard them and bustled up with an outraged "Nah, then! Wot's all this?"

My friend smiled at the memory. "Picture it," he said. "This innocent, pink-cheeked boy, reprehending unknown to himself the *Lord Chief Justice* and the *Lord Chancellor*! It's the most beautiful left-and-right in the history of English field sports!"

Hervey Allen, the author of *Anthony Adverse*, told me that the word *kibosh* means "the black cap of death"; hence "to put the kibosh on" someone is to sentence him to death. I learn from *A Companion to Murder*, by E. Spencer Shew, that a Queen's Bench judge trying criminal cases "carries white gloves and Black Cap, a square of limp black silk dating from the early 16th century which was formerly laid corner-wise on the judge's wig when he passed sentence of death"—a kibosh? It is originally a Gaelic word, Allen said, but Webster disagrees—"perh. of Yiddish origin."

The House of Lords passed the vital Habeas Corpus Act in 1679 by a majority of two, and then only because a light-hearted tally clerk counted an unusually fat peer as the equivalent of ten men.

In Scottish law, the second-born of twins is considered the senior, and if they are males, and a title is at stake, he is its inheritor, as he is believed to have been the first conceived.

Lightning Calculators

Oscar Verhaege (b. 1862), a Belgian, squared 888,888,888,888,888 in 40 seconds, without pen and paper. Later he raised 9,999,999 to the fifth power in 60 seconds; the answer ran to 35 digits.

Truman Henry Stafford (b. 1836), an American, was asked to square 365,365,365,365,365,365, and "in no more than one minute" gave the answer: 133,491,850,208,566,925,016, 658,299,941,583,225. Stafford was ten years old at the time.

Zerah Colburn (b. 1804), also an American, was challenged to raise 8 to the sixteenth power and "in a few seconds" gave the answer: 281,474,976,710,656. Colburn was eight years old.

Johan Dase of Hamburg (b. 1824) multiplied 2 numbers of 20 digits each in 6 minutes, 2 of 40 digits in 40 minutes, and 2 of 100 digits in 8 hours and 45 minutes.

Jedediah Buxton of Derbyshire (b. 1707) specialized in interpreting the infinitely large in terms of the infinitesimally small, such as: How many human hairs could be contained in a cubic mile? Answer: 586,040,972,673,024,000. And how many cubic eighths of an inch are there in a rectangular block of stone 23,145,789 yards long by 5,642,732 wide by 54,965 thick? (Never mind the answer to *that* one!) Buxton had another, more useful talent: He could glance at a field, however irregular its shape, and almost instantly announce a minutely accurate estimate of its acreage.

Rex Stout, the creator of Nero Wolfe, shared Buxton's gift for instantaneous estimate. As a child, he gave exhibitions in which he would glance at a column of figures and immediately announce the total.

Again like Buxton, George Parker Bidder of Derbyshire (b. 1806) dealt with the infinite/infinitesimal. How many hogsheads of cider could be pressed from 1,000,000 apples if 30 apples yield 1 quart? The ten-year-old boy gave the correct answer in 35 seconds: 132 hogsheads, 17 gallons, and 1 quart, with 10 apples over. At twelve, told that a pendulum oscillated 9¾ inches per second, he was asked how far it would travel in 7 years, 14 days, 2 hours, 1 minute, and 56 seconds, allowing 365 days, 5 hours, 48 minutes, and 55 seconds to a year. He gave the answer in less than a minute: 2,165,625,744¾ inches.

Final note: All these freaks were *men*. Not a woman among them.

Literature Quiz

(ANSWERS ON NEXT PAGE)

1. Some of the best-known verses in English are by authors whose names are almost totally unknown to even the educated public. For instance, who wrote:
   a. "Annie Laurie."
   b. "Mary Had a Little Lamb."
   c. "Twinkle, Twinkle Little Star."
2. "The Three Bears" (and "Goldilocks") is by an author well known for his poems but hardly at all for his prose. Who is he?
3. Who said:
   a. God tempers the wind . . . to the shorn lamb.
   b. It is a far, far better thing that I do now, etc.
   c. Quick, Watson, the needle!
4. Who was Lothario?
5. Name the short story by W. Somerset Maugham that was dramatized as *Rain*.
6. Identify ".007."
7. Who wrote the lyric to the popular song "Bill"?
8. Name three works of fiction in which an important character is often mentioned but never appears.
9. *Moby Dick, or The Whale* is the full title of Melville's novel. Name the main titles of the works of which the secondary titles follow:
   a. *Life Among the Lowly.*
   b. *The Preacher*.
   c. *What You Will.*
   d. *The Mistakes of a Night.*
   e. *The Parish Boy's Progress.*
   f. *The Modern Prometheus*.
10. What was the real name of Mr. Dick in *David Copperfield?*
11. Johann Rudolf Wyss wrote one of the best loved of all books for children. What is it?
12. Who wrote the poem "St. Agnes' Eve"?

LITERATURE QUIZ *(Answers)*

1. a. William Douglas.
   b. Sarah Josepha Hale.
   c. Jane Taylor.
2. Robert Southey.
3. a. Laurence Sterne, in *A Sentimental Journey*.
   b. Not Sydney Carton, in *A Tale of Two Cities*. At th beginning of the passage, Dickens writes, "If [Syd ney Carton] had given any utterance to hi [thoughts], they . . . would have been these." But h didn't.
   c. Not Sherlock Holmes, contrary to popular belief Nor did he anywhere say, "Elementary, my dea Watson!"
4. A libertine in *The Fair Penitent*, by Nicholas Rowe 1703.
5. "Miss Thompson."
6. A locomotive in Kipling's short story of that name. James Bond was "007."
7. P. G. Wodehouse.
8. Mrs. Grundy, in *Speed the Plough*, by Tom Morton; Mrs. Harris (Sairey Gamp's friend), in *Martin Chuzzle-wit*, by Dickens; Bunbury, in *The Importance of Being Earnest*, by Oscar Wilde.
9. a. *Uncle Tom's Cabin*.
   b. Ecclesiastes.
   c. *Twelfth Night*.
   d. *She Stoops to Conquer*.

e. *Oliver Twist*.
f. *Frankenstein*.

10. Richard Babley.
11. *The Swiss Family Robinson*.
12. Tennyson. Keats's poem is called "The Eve of St. Agnes."

London

If you happen to need a sword-stick, go to James Smith & Sons, 53 New Oxford Street.

Behind the Royal Exchange is a statue of an American millionaire, George Peabody, who gave great sums of money toward clearing London slums. He died in 1869, and his body was returned to his native town, South Danvers, Massachusetts, which thereupon changed its name to Peabody.

The court at the entrance to the Savoy Hotel is the only place in London where traffic keeps to the right.

A plaque in Pickering Place, just off St. James's Street, marks the location (1842–45) of the "Legation for the Ministers from the Republic of Texas to the Court of St. James's." The last duel in London is said to have been fought here.

In July 1936, an Irish journalist, George McMahon, made a half-hearted attempt to assassinate King Edward VIII on Constitution Hill, at almost the identical spot where Edward Oxford had tried to assassinate Queen Victoria in June 1840.

The top-hatted, uniformed beadles in the Burlington Arcade, which is privately owned, are there to see that you don't (among other things) whistle on the premises, or sing, or run, or carry a large parcel or an open umbrella.

The Mayflower pub on Rotherhithe Street (pronounced "Redriff") has the unique privilege of selling both English and American postage stamps. This was granted originally as a convenience for sailors, but it continues as a bonbon for tourists come to see where the *Mayflower* sailed from, to pick up the Pilgrims at Plymouth.

Contrary to popular belief, Marylebone takes its name from St. Mary-le-Bourne—St. Mary's Brook—not from Mary La Bonne.

Wonderful, mysterious, grand, clever old London, who keeps the Ritz Hotel front-door closed on Sundays and the side-door open!

LADY NORAH BENTINCK,
My Wanderings and Memories

Underneath London lie twelve abandoned railway stations.

The first cotton crop in America was grown from seed sent from the Chelsea Physick Gardens.

Some of the money that John Harvard devoted to founding the college, he obtained from the sale of the Queen's Head Inn, near London Bridge. Downing Street, the official address of the Prime Minister, was built by and named for a Harvard graduate, Sir George Downing.

London, that great cesspool into which all the loungers of the Empire are irresistibly drained.

SIR ARTHUR CONAN DOYLE, *A Study in Scarlet*

London, the great wen.

WILLIAM COBBETT

A liveryman of Goldsmiths' Hall has two precious privileges: He may not be arrested for drunkenness in the borough of London, and if he is sentenced to be hanged, he may choose a silken cord instead of a hempen rope.

The largest clock in London—that is, the one with the largest *dial*—is not Big Ben, which is only 22½ feet in diameter, but the clock on top of Shell-Mex House, which is 26 feet. In fact, Big Ben is not a clock at all, but the bell that rings the hours.

London Notices

At 30 Eaton Place: QUITE OUTSTANDING FLAT FOR SALE.

On a road in Regents Park: REVERSE CAMBER.

In Victoria Street: NO ENTRY EXCEPT FOR ACCESS.

In Lloyds Bank, Berkeley Square, where the path to the counters is laid out with a velvet rope: WAY IN. PLEASE WAIT OTHERSIDE.

Over a shop in (I think) Westover Terrace (I couldn't read the street sign clearly): JOHN P. DAVIS AND, BY THE GRACE OF GOD, HIS EIGHT CHILDREN.

In a shop window on Conduit Street: "CATHEDRAL ANALYSIS."

Formerly in the lavatory of the Reading Room at the British Museum: CASUAL ABLUTIONS ONLY. (Some visitors had been doing their laundry there.)

My favorite shop name: WHELPDALE, MAXWELL & CODD.

On a counter in a branch of the Westminster Bank: TILL CLOSED.

At the entrance to a short cul-de-sac: UNSUITABLE FOR LONG VEHICLES.

In Sloane Street: HEEL BAR. (I saw this from the top of a bus which moved on before I could make out what the sign represented. I surmise it was a cobbler's shop, but I don't know.)

John Steinbeck was delighted to find a small tin box of mints in London, advertised on the cover as "curiously strong." He liked to offer them around with "Care to try a curiously strong?"

In the district known as Little Venice: BEWARE OF THE DOGE.

On the shoulder of a high-crowned suburban road: SOFT VERGES.

In Sackville Street, a shop selling ornate bathroom fixtures: PLUSH FLUSH.

In a public garden in Belgravia:

LADIES AND GENTLEMEN WILL NOT,
OTHERS MUST NOT,
PICK THE FLOWERS.

A sign reported on a local [London] church:

ARE YE WEARY OF SIN?
COME IN AND REST

Below it was written in pencil: IF NOT, CALL 123-4567.

Malta

Malta is:

> "The key that commands Egypt."—NAPOLEON
> "The direct road to Sicily."—LORD NELSON
> "The bar to Africa."—HITLER

Malta's soil is so shallow that farmers still use primitive wooden ploughs, and so scanty that visiting ships once paid their harbor fees in loads of earth. Yet the local figs, oranges, nectarines, peaches, and apricots are among the finest in the world.

Because about half the population is illiterate, the motor buses are painted in different colors, according to their routes.

One of Malta's principal products is lace. Queen Victoria once ordered "8 doz. pr. long and 8 doz. pr. short mitts." And one of its "crops" is wild birds, netted for the market.

Venerable riddle: "How do you make a Maltese cross?" Answer: "Step on its tail."

The average Maltese eats from two to three pounds of bread a day.

St. Paul and St. Luke were shipwrecked here in A.D. 60 and lived in a grotto, where St. Luke painted a picture of the Virgin and Child on a wall.

There was a young lady of Malta
Who strangled her aunt with a halter.
She said, "I won't bury her;
She'll do for my terrier;
She'll keep for a month if I salt her."

Anon.

Malta was the home and headquarters of the Knights of St. John of Jerusalem (a.k.a. the Knights of Malta) from 1530 until 1798. Their imprint is still deep upon the island, especially in the Co-Cathedral of St. John, in Valletta. Once it was the richest church in Christendom. Today it still dazzles, with its jewels and precious metals and paintings and marbles. The loot that Napoleon's troops carried off included a lamp and chain that melted down to 172 pounds of solid gold. They missed the gates of the Chapel of the Blessed Sacrament, which are of solid silver, six feet tall. The churchmen had painted them black, and the looters mistook them for common iron.

Emigrants from Malta to the U.S. settle mostly in Detroit.

The Maltese consider the sight of the human navel dangerously inflammatory. None is allowed to appear in a newspaper photograph or a magazine illustration.

The armory of the Palace of the Grand Masters of the Knights has the world's finest collection of arms and armor —some 7,600 pieces, including a helmet weighing forty-seven pounds. Seeing it, you realize that the stairs in the palace have three-inch risers for the benefit not only of gouty dignitaries but also of iron-burdened warriors.

Because of Malta's heroism in World War II, King George VI of Great Britain awarded the George Cross to the entire population. If you wish to send a letter to someone in Malta, the address should end "Malta, G.C."

At the peak of the tourist season, Malta claims to have one visitor for every citizen (pop. about 320,000).

Among the prehistoric bones found on Malta are those of a pygmy elephant and a gigantic dormouse.

The stone of the [Maltese] rocks, and therefore of the houses, has a beautiful golden tint, which, with the intense blue of the surrounding Mediterranean, makes the island look like a topaz set in sapphires.

HENRY HOLIDAY, *Reminiscences of My Life*

Medicine

Dr. Alexis Carrel, the famous surgeon, could put his forefinger and his middle finger into an ordinary matchbox with a short length of catgut and tie a knot in it.

I once knew an obstetrician who established a reputation for infallible predictions. When a prospective mother asked him which sex her baby would be, he asked, "What do you want?" Whatever she answered, he told her, "Fine! That's what it will be. I'll make a note of it now," and wrote in his notebook the opposite of what he had promised. So, if she had asked for a boy and got one, he told her smugly, "See? Just what I said." But if the baby was a girl, he'd say, "Just what I promised. See? I wrote it down"—and he'd show her the note.

They taught in the XVI century that a child could suffer neither heat nor cold all his life if his hand had been rubbed with juice of wormwood before his 12th birthday.

J. K. HUYSMANS, *Down There*

Nothing comes out of the human body that can't be washed away with soap and water.

One of Queen Victoria's "sovereign remedies" was rolling in the grass. That, or what she delicately called "an opening medicine," was her prescription for most ills.

Dr. Oliver Wendell Holmes spoke of cancer as "the shark's tooth."

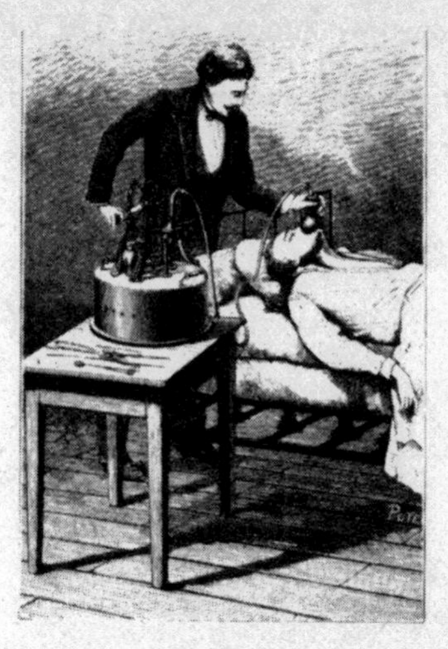

British surgeons are addressed as "Mister," not "Doctor."

I've got Bright's disease, and he's got mine.

S. J. PERELMAN

There is iron enough in the blood of 42 men to make a ploughshare weighing 24 pounds. A Scotch writer had remarked that this fact is not so wonderful when it is considered that there is as much *flint* in the hearts of some men as would serve the firelocks of 42 soldiers!

JOSEPH HAYDN, *Dictionary of Dates*

The energy given out by the hands of healers is an electromagnetic wave whose length is approximately 22 cm.

Journal of the British Society of Dowsers, vol. xi, no. 83

To ward off a sprain, Cato the Elder would repeat over and over, "*Hauat hauat hauat ista pista sista damnia bodannaustra.*"

THEODOR MOMMSEN, *History of Rome*

The Rev. James Woodforde (1740–1803) believed that a stye could be relieved by rubbing it with the tail of a black cat, and that if a cat washed both her ears, the weather would change.

Memory

My own memory... was perhaps what might be called a fairly good one. Of its enfeeblement in certain ways I am fully conscious.... The names of familiar persons and things are now frequently forgotten or not readily recalled. The mind often halts even as to common words; and recovers them in the end not by any effort of will, but by some sudden and almost impulsive suggestion. Recent events and dates are easily lost or pass into confusion, while those of long prior time still hold firm root and their right place in remembrance.

SIR HENRY HOLLAND, *Recollections of Past Life*

It's enough to throw you into despair: to read everything, and remember nothing! Because you do remember nothing. You may strain as much as you like: everything escapes. Here and there a few tatters remain, fragile as those puffs of smoke left over after a train has passed.

JULES RENARD, *Journal*

That I can be happy while I am reading, is a great blessing. Could I have remembered, as some men do, what I have read, I should have been able to call myself an educated man. But that power I have never possessed. Something is always left,—something dim and inaccurate,—but still something sufficient to preserve the taste for more. I am inclined to think that it is so with most readers.

THOMAS ADOLPHUS TROLLOPE, *What I Remember*

The actor Charles Macklin (1697–1797) boasted that he could recite anything after one reading, so Samuel Foote composed "An Incoherent Story" and challenged him with it:

"She went into the garden to cut a cabbage-leaf, to make an apple pie; and at the same time, a great she-bear, coming up the street, pops its head into the shop. 'What! no soap?' so he died, and she very imprudently married the barber; and there were present the Picninnies, the Joblillies, and the Garyalies, and the grand Panjandrum himself with the little round button at top."

This is the version given in the *Oxford Book of Quotations*, but there is another, which continues, "And they danced until the gunpowder ran out at the heels of their boots." Whether or not Macklin made good his boast, I don't know.

Cyrus the Great could address every soldier in his army by name.

Léon Gambetta (1838–82), the French statesman, could recite every word by Rabelais ever published, and could quote thousands of pages of Victor Hugo *verbatim*, and recite the Book of Ruth backward.

Mathurin Versierre of Prussia could listen to twelve different sentences in twelve different languages, all strange to him, and repeat them syllable for syllable.

Theodore Hook could recite all the advertisements in the *Times* of London after one reading and name in order all the shops along Oxford Street.

H. L. Mencken's brother August could recall something he did on every day of his mature life.

Elijah ben Solomon Zalman, the Gaon of Vilna, memorized 2,500 books.

Pierre Mouchon (1733–97), a Genovois, memorized all seventeen volumes of the *Encyclopédie*: some 18,000,000 words.

All my life, as down an abyss without a bottom, I have been pouring van-loads of information into that vacancy of oblivion I call my mind.

LOGAN PEARSALL SMITH, *All Trivia*

Almost twenty years since, I heard a profane jest, and still remember it. How many pious passages of a far later date have I forgotten! It seems my soul is like a filthy pond, wherein fish die soon, and frogs live long.

DR. THOMAS FULLER, *Introductio ad Prudentiam*

Macaulay could memorize a whole play of Shakespeare's in one evening and could recite the whole of *Paradise Lost*.

Memory is the greatest of artists, and effaces from your mind what is unnecessary.

MAURICE BARING, *Have You Anything to Declare?*

I find that the further back I go, the better I remember things, whether they happened or not.

MARK TWAIN

Miscellaneous

Why does one never hear of a *blessing* thundering down the years and pursuing a certain family while pouring the gifts of the gods into their laps?

LADY NORAH BENTINCK,
My Wanderings and Memories

Every man thinks meanly of himself for not having been a soldier, or not having been at sea.

SAMUEL JOHNSON

Placing him [a shy boy] at a public school is forcing an owl upon day.

IB.

There is no absurdity so palpable but that it can be planted firmly in the human head if only you begin to inculcate it before the age of five, by constantly repeating it with an air of great solemnity.

SCHOPENHAUER

However gradual the course of history, there must always be the day, even an hour or minute, when some significant action is performed for the first or the last time.

PETER QUENNELL, *The Singular Preference*

Would you trust him enough to go to sleep with your finger in his mouth?

DWIGHT MORROW

Two unforgettable addresses, valid until recently: The Duke of Wellington's, Number 1, London; and Blaine Littell's, the Garden of Gethsemane, Jerusalem.

Though everything is not permitted, everything is possible.

ROGER BACON

Murphy's Law—"If anything can go wrong, it will"—should be extended as follows: "and usually late on a Friday afternoon."

[John Worta (alias Bellini, Balbidson, Charnovich and Count Kastriot-Albansky) wrote in his suicide note to Elizabeth Chudleigh, the Duchess of Kingston, in 1784:] "I have learned the deportment of a prince, although my father was an ass-driver at Trebizond."

ELIZABETH MAVOR, *The Virgin Mistress*

The six most important words are: "I admit I made a mistake." The five most important words are: "You did a good job." The four most important words are: "What is your opinion?" The three most important words are: "If you please." The two most important words are: "Thank you." The *least* important word is: "I."

BRIG. GEN. JACKSON ROZIER, USA

Sir William Harcourt [Home Secretary under Gladstone], when telephoned by a bore, would pour ink into the receiver, secure in the belief... that it would trickle into either the ear or the mouth of his inquisitor.

KENNETH ROSE, *Superior Person*

Australia is said to have roughly the same number of sheep as the United States has people, and roughly the same number of people as the United States has sheep.

Pauline Bonaparte, Napoleon's sister, could turn her ears inside out by muscular control, without touching them.

In 1958, the Atomic Energy Commission proposed that clairvoyants be employed in an attempt to foretell where Russian bombs would fall in the event of war.

Report of the Rand Commission, August 31, 1958

The great Indian mathematician Srinivasa Ramanujan lived in a world of numbers. Shorly before his death in 1920, at the age of thirty, he was visited by the great English mathematician G. H. Hardy, who happened to mention that he had arrived in a taxi with the license 1729. Ramanujan exclaimed, "What a wonderful number! It is the lowest number that can be expressed in two ways as the sum of two cubes." (Viz., $12^3 + 1^3$, and $10^3 + 9^3$)

Most dowsers cannot carry a watch without its stopping.

If I were examining a class in English composition, I would ask them to explain, clearly and succinctly, how to tie a bowknot.

Silk hats and derbies, detachable cuffs, sleeve garters, dickeys, scarf pins, spats, piping on waistcoats, pince-nez, watch fobs and watch chains and watch charms, celluloid collars, the male pompadour, white-flannel trousers, and gold-headed walking sticks: Where are they now? Gone with the mashie niblick and the nose guard.

Sinister notice from the Credit Card Service Bureau: "YOU ARE CURRENTLY DUE TO EXPIRE 11/86."

Bernard Shaw referred to apostrophes as "uncouth bacilli" and argued that one should be used only when omitting it would lead to confusion with another word, as *hell* and *he'll*, *wont* and *won't*.

J. McC., of his wife: "She cried, 'I'm *exhausted*!' and flung her arms wide, squandering on the gesture enough energy to have carried her through the day."

When a professional magician dies, it is traditional for his wand to be broken over his casket by a colleague.

A popular jingle in the Royal Australian Navy is

> Never go out on deck at night,
> Crossing the Great Australian Bight!

Unpopular officers have been known simply to disappear, and the man-eating sharks that are thick in the bight make sure that no one jettisoned survives.

J. G. is a powerful stimulus to memory. He has only to join a group for everyone in it to remember an urgent engagement elsewhere.

I have an invitation from Madame de Lignerole in these words—"Will you be so very kind as to allow me to take the liberty of entreating you to have the kindness to confer the favour upon me of giving me the happiness of your company on Friday?"

AUGUSTUS J. C. HARE, *The Story of My Life*

Inscription in the library at Murcia, Spain: "Here the dead open the eyes of the living."

In the first split second of making contact with a stranger—that is, before our intellect and logic have time to start work—then we may well receive an accurate first impression, due solely to intuition.

FREDRICK MARION, *In My Mind's Eye*

Two things you never see: a one-legged Chinese man and a dead white mule.

The stories of childhood leave an indelible impression, and their author always has a niche in the temple of memory from which the image is never cast out to be thrown on the rubbish heap of things that are outgrown and outlived.

HOWARD PYLE

. . . the uncritical and unquestioning loyalty that we most of us pay to books read out to us in childhood and endeared to us by the remembered voice that introduced their delights.

JOHN GORE, "Saki"

Back in the 1950s, some sensitive documents were stolen from the American Embassy in one of the Balkan countries. I saw the dispatch reporting the theft, and I have treasured it ever since as an example of the purest official gibberish. It ended "PENETRATION IS BELIEVED TO HAVE BEEN EFFECTUATED BY INDIGENOUS JANITORIAL PERSONNEL." That is, they think the janitor done it.

The original purpose of those handsome silk sashes worn by officer cadets at West Point was to serve as an emergency hammock for carrying the wounded. The reputed origin of the aiguillette is even more curious: In the sixteenth century the Duke of Alba made every soldier wear a stout noose around his left shoulder, so that if he quailed in battle, he could be hanged on the spot.

The U.S. Mint once issued a penny piece which was known as the "Franklin cent," after the philosopher who had suggested the motto it bore: MIND YOUR BUSINESS.

Washington is full of the most attractive men—and the women they married when they were young.

Anon.

The Great Wall of China, alone among artifacts on earth, is visible from near space.

When G. K. Chesterton first saw Times Square at night, he said, "How thrilling it would be, if only one couldn't read!"

Part of Leonard Woolf's duties as a civil servant in Ceylon was signing death warrants. This so horrified him that it left him with shaking hands; he was unable to knot a necktie and thereafter wore it through a ring.

GEORGE ORWELL?

I think so, but I'm not sure. I hope some reader will inform me.

"Argent on gules a mayd stark naked with a chaplet in her hand dexter." John Aubrey is the authority for ascribing this remarkable coat of arms not only to a Doctor of Divinity, but to the Dean of St. Paul's no less, "*tempore Henrici VII*," with the appealing name Dr. Innocent.

One night Milnes chanced to sleep at the Wakefield Asylum where he had attended a meeting. . . . "It was a curious sensation, sleeping under the same roof as 1,500 lunatics. I was kept awake by thoughts of the *kind of sleep* that was going on about me."

T. WEMYSS REID, *Life & Letters of Richard Monckton Milnes, Lord Houghton*

Of the 633 officers and men aboard Nelson's flagship *Victory* at Trafalgar, 22 were Americans.

Hectare is an anagram for *the acre*.

Bishop Heinrich of Belgium (fl. 1281) fathered sixty-one children.

A curious anticipation of the airplane: "You will be necessarily upbourne by the air, if you can renew any impulse upon it faster than the air can recede from the pressure."

SAMUEL JOHNSON, *Rasselas* (1759)

Given: A pair of scales and 8 balls, identical except that one is heavier than the others. *Problem*: To identify it in 2 weighings. *Solution*: Set any two balls aside, and weigh the others 3, and 3. If they balance, weigh the other two, 1 against 1. If they don't balance, discard all three in the light pan of the scales; put aside any 1 of the other three, and weigh the remaining two, 1 against 1.

King George V, on being told that an officer of his acquaintance was a homosexual: "I thought that men like that shot themselves."

Lord Wemyss, a delightful old gentleman of ninety, had a "Mona Lisa" which he insisted was the real one. The one in the Louvre, he said, was a copy. We were all polite and agreed with him.

ETHEL BARRYMORE, *Memories*

Nature gives you the face you have at twenty. Life shapes the face you have at thirty. But at fifty you get the face you deserve.

COCO CHANEL

Mnemonics

For remembering *pi* to 14 places: "How I want a drink, champagne or Scotch, after the heavy chapters involving quantum mechanics"—i.e., 3.14159265358979.

WILLY LEY

And "Can I remember the reciprocal?" gives the reciprocal: 0.318310.

For remembering on which side to pass a buoy: *Red right returning*, and

Black to port,
Back to port.

Also, *port* wine is red; and there are four letters in *port* and *left*.

For remembering the battles in the Wars of the Roses: the initial letters of "A black Negress was my aunt: there's her house behind the barn."

GEORGE ORWELL, "Such, Such Were the Joys"

For distinguishing between:

A *stalactite* and a *stalagmite*: Little mites grow up.

Continuous and *continual*: A clock ticks continually, whereas most rivers are *sinuous*, and all flow *continuously.*

Stationery and *stationary*: A stationEry shop sells Erasers and Envelopes.

Supine and *prone*: Face Up is sUPine.

The Royal Families of Britain, from the Conquest on: The initial letters of "Neighbors Persuaded Lovely Yvonne To Shut Her Window"—Norman, Plantagenet, Lancaster, York, Tudor, Stuart, Hanover, Windsor.

Finally, the most useless piece of information in this whole book: a mnemonic for remembering the order of cases in declensions in Serbo-Croat: No Good Is Done After Violence In Love or Passion—Nominative, Genitive, Dative, Accusative, Vocative, Instrumental, Locative or Prepositional.

Music and Musicians

[Alphonse Bertillon, the great French criminologist, and Captain Horatio Hornblower, the hero of the fictional series by C.S. Forester, were utterly tone-deaf. When Bertillon did his military service, he had to count the bugle notes in order to distinguish one call from another. As for Hornblower,] One tune was the same as another . . . and the most beautiful music was to him no more than comparable to the noise of a cart along a gravel road.

C. S. FORESTER, *Ship of the Line*

Although the Rt. Rev. H. St. George Tucker, late Presiding Bishop of the Episcopal Church, was quite as tone-deaf as these two, he joined in every hymn, always singing it to the tune of "There Is a Green Hill Far Away," the only one he could carry.

Jascha Heifetz's sister, Pauline (Mrs. Samuel Chotzinoff), had such perfect pitch that she could turn her back to a piano and invite you to strike the keyboard with your fist, then call off every key you had struck.

Bozo's Gypsy Quartet played sagging Serbian melodies full of glissandos and vibratos and long slimy arpeggios.

LAWRENCE DURRELL, "Call of the Sea"

Claudio Arrau memorized enough music to give forty recitals of 2½ hours each.

Giuseppe Verdi has the distinction among composers of having had his name become a political slogan. During Italy's struggle for union in the 1850s, patriots attending performances of his operas would shout "Verdi! Verdi!"—a convenient acronym for *Vittorio Emanuele Re D'Italia*.

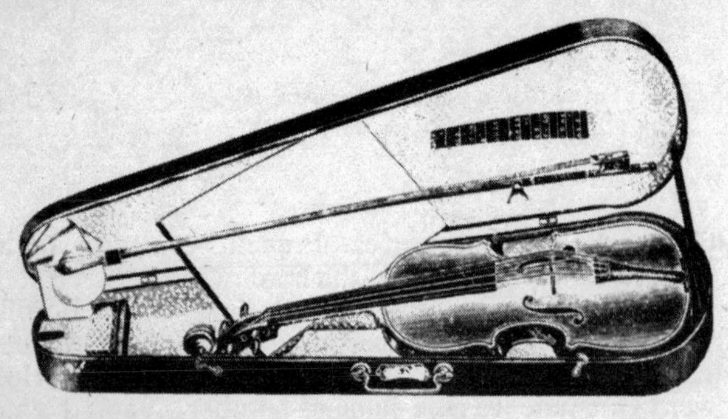

The infant Jenny Lind's first cry is said to have been F in alt. When Bishop Stanley of Norwich heard her sing "Angels Ever Bright and Fair," he said, "What beautiful words! If only you would say them, without the notes!"

Classic music is th' kind that we keep thinkin' 'll turn into a tune.

KIN HUBBARD, *Abe Martin*

Gustave Doré, the French artist, put over the entrance to his villa: Do, Mi, Si, La, Do, Re—"*Domicile à Doré*."

Which reminds me that a lady once showed me her gold cigarette case, engraved with a bar of music that translated thus: LA MI DO CI LA LA DO RE, or *L'ami docile à l'adorée*, or "The submissive friend, to the adored one."

An air played on the bagpipes, with that detestable, monotonous drone of theirs for the bass, is like a tune tied to a post.

LEIGH HUNT

In the Solomon Islands, the pidgin English for *piano* is *bokkis yupala hittim i tok*—"box-you-hit-him-he-talks."

Two American sisters, Mildred and Patty Hill, wrote *and copyrighted* (in 1893) the words of music of one of the most popular songs in the world, "Happy Birthday."

There is a spirituality about the face, however . . . which the typewriter does not generate. The lady is a musician.

SIR ARTHUR CONAN DOYLE, "The Solitary Cyclist"

The Syrian general Nicator fainted at the sound of a flute.

The Russian horn music was invented by Prince Galitzin in 1762. This instrument consisted of forty persons, "*whose life is spent in blowing one note*." This, to be sure, is sounding the very "bass-note of humility." A man converted into a crochet! An A-flat in the sixtieth year of his age! A fellow creature of Alfred and Epaminondas, he has passed his life in acting a semitone! in waiting for his turn to exist, and then seizing the desperate instant, and being a puff!

LEIGH HUNT, "Russian Horn Band"

Gioacchino Rossini (1792–1868), who is best known for his *William Tell Overture*, used to wear three wigs in winter, to keep his head warm.

Madame Bizet, then a young girl of only fifteen, was getting ready to take her first piano lesson with [Gounod] when he said to her: "Arch your wrists and make a *lilac* note in which I can wash my hands."

Paris and the Arts, 1851–1896, from the *Goncourt Journal*

Mrs. Amy Beach (1867–1944) was the first American woman to compose a symphony. Her Gaelic Symphony was performed by the Boston Symphony in 1896.

It is extraordinary how potent cheap music is.

NOËL COWARD

Mozart, at the age of two, heard a pig squeal and announced, "G-sharp!" Someone went to a piano and struck a G-sharp. The child was right.

Vienna has a tablet to a citizen who was humble yet world-renowned. His name was Augustin, and you'd identify him at once if I could whistle seven notes for you, the opening notes of a bouncy little waltz. The words that go with them are "*Ach, du lieber Augustin!*" Not only did Augustin really live, but he became a local celebrity in the great plague of 1679. Hence the tablet.

Another waltz, equally famous, is "Chopsticks." Why the name "Chopsticks"? The French title, "Côtelettes," adds to the mystery. (The German is similar: "Koteletten Walzer.") In 1880 four famous Russian composers—Borodin, Cui, Liadov and Rimsky-Korsakov—published their "Paraphrases for Four Hands at One Piano," a series of twenty-two variations on the "Chopsticks" theme. Liszt was so taken with them that he contributed another variation to the second edition.

"My Idea of Heaven Is"—

—to be drawn in an easy coach on a smooth turf, with easy descents and declivities.

EDMUND BURKE

—to sit in a garden and receive news by alternate messengers of British victories on land.

ALFRED AUSTIN

—eating pâtés de foie gras to the sound of trumpets.

SYDNEY SMITH

—to be in a perfect automobile going thirty miles an hour on a smooth road to a twelfth-century cathedral.

ELIZABETH STEVENSON, *Henry Adams, a Biography*

—to take two stiff drinks of good whiskey and go to bed and read something I myself have written.

CAPTAIN WILLIAM H. ROYALL, C.S.A.

—to sit for placid hours under a lotus tree eating of ice creams and pelican pie, with our feet in a hazure coloured stream and with the birds and beasts of Paradise a sporting around us.

EDWARD LEAR

(He also said, "I shall stipulate that I shall only go into Heaven on condition that I am never in a room with more than ten people.")

A Book of Verses underneath the Bough,
A Jug of Wine, A Loaf of Bread—and Thou
Beside me singing in the Wilderness—
Oh, Wilderness were Paradise enow!

EDWARD FITZGERALD,
Rubáiyát of Omar Khayyám

(Some cynic amended the second line to "—and fifty thou.")

—to live in a palace whose furnishings and décor would be in a continual state of change and replacement, while outside in formal gardens would be rare fountains and ancient statues, also being constantly moved about.

COUNT BONI DE CASTELLANE, quoted in
Cornelia Otis Skinner, *Elegant Wits and Grand Horizontals*

If he'd had no duties and no reference to posterity, Dr. Johnson would have spent his life driving briskly in a post chaise with a pretty woman.

Names

The longest one-word place-name in the U.S. Postal Directory is Charlottesville, the seat of the University of Virginia.

I once had the privilege of introducing Mr. Lee Grant to Mrs. Lincoln Davis—the opposing Civil War generals to the opposing Civil War presidents.

Names that seem to fit their owners perfectly: Chief Superintendent Hawkyard, of Scotland Yard; Flinders Petrie, Egyptologist and archaeologist; Foxhall Keene, famous horseman and all-round athlete; Beilby Porteous, Bishop of London; Slade Cutter, former football coach at the U.S. Naval Academy; General Sir Bindon Blood.

What has happened to those snotty, Newporty names like Reginald, Algernon, Montmorency, Percival, Marmaduke, Archibald, Chauncey? You never hear them anymore. And who is coming along to take the place of the Wyllys Rossiter Bettses, the F. Skiddy von Stades, and the Norman de R. Whitehouses, the George B. St. Georges, the E. von der Horst Kochs, and the Fal de Saint-Phalles—names which once shone with such refulgence from the pages of *Spur* and *Town Topics*? Mrs. C. Bai Lihme and Mrs. S. Stanwood Menken, who has inherited your richly rustling mantles?

All family trees lose themselves among the Smiths. If ants have names for each other, they must use a tiny equivalent for Smith.

WILLIAM BOLITHO

A cockney tried to name Hepworth, Ontario, after Epworth, England.

The middle initial in the names of Harry S Truman, Owen D Young and Fiorello H LaGuardia stood for nothing.

A perfect example of a round peg in a round hole is a certain filling station operator in Hatteras, N.C.: Wheeler Ballance. I like to think that he has a partner named Philip Tanks.

"C. Z." Guest (Mrs. Winston Guest) was christened Lucy. The "C.Z." represents her younger brother's attempt to say "Sister."

How to invent names for fictitious characters without fear of prosecution? This morning's *Times* [of London] has births to Clague, Fimbel, Futty and Prescott-Pickup.

The Diaries of Evelyn Waugh

People claiming their names had been used in the news burlesques, and that they had been held up to ridicule, were always threatening to sue. To eliminate this annoyance, we invented a set of names . . . like Tomtit McGee, Beau Bernstein, Falvey Nishball. I thought we were safe until one summer up in Maine, an old gentleman stopped me and said, "Mr. Allen, I heard my name on your program last winter. Who sent it in to you?"

"What is your name?"

"Sinbad Brittle."

FRED ALLEN, Condensed from *Treadmill to Oblivion*

Back in the 1920s one of the New York papers asked its readers to send in what they considered the most interesting personal name they had ever encountered. The winner was a Mr. Pleasant Finch.

A sister of [A. Conan] Doyle's married a clergyman named Angel. Next door to them lived another clergyman, named

Dam. And later on Dam was moved to Goring, and found himself next door to a priest whose name was Father Hell. Providence, I take it, arranges these things for some wise purpose.

JEROME K. JEROME, *My Life and Times*

The name of the town of Hossegor, near Biarritz, commemorates the billeting there, during the Napoleonic Wars, of Wellington's Horse Guards.

Have you ever noticed how many villains have names containing the letters A, I and N, in that order? For instance: Stalin, Cain, Fagin, Tarquin, Catiline, Ivan (the Terrible), Idi Amin, Catherine (de'Medici), Damien (who tried to assassinate Louis XV in 1757), Rasputin—not to mention the word *villain* itself? (But how about Washington and Franklin?)

A small, special category of names:

Charles James Fox, prime minister
Frank Lloyd Wright, architect
John Horne Tooke, philologist
Lynn Bogue Hunt, illustrator
James Wong Howe, cameraman
Charles Hoy Fort, incrediblist
John George Brown, painter
John Ross Roach, hockey star
John Paul Jones, admiral
James Earl Jones, actor
James Knox Polk, president
Sun Yat Sen, statesman
Clare Boothe Luce, ambassadress
Guy Bates Post, actor
George Platt Lynes, photographer
John Wilkes Booth, assassin.

There is a city named A in Sweden and a bay named Y in the Zuyder Zee. France has a village named Ws, a river named As, and a lake and a town named Oo.

Many actors change their original names to ones more eu-
phonious or romantic or elegant; many writers adopt *noms
de plume*; prize fighters, *noms de ring*; and rock singers
noms de mike. We are quite used to this little practice. But
was surprised to learn how many great painters and sculp-
tors had done the same thing and that in many cases th
names I knew them by were actually nicknames or sobr
quets. Most of these names fall into two classes: Eithe
they tell where the owner was born, or they are descriptive

Among the first and best known are El Greco, "th
Greek," whose real name was, of course, Domenicos Theo
tocopouli; Perugino, "a son of Perugia," was Pietro
Christoforo Vannucci; and Sassoferrato, who was bor
there, began life as Giovanni Battista Salvi.

The second group includes Tintoretto, "Little Dyer," be
cause that was his father's profession (his real name wa
Jacopo Robusti); Masaccio, "Slovenly Tom" or "Hulkin
Tom," originally Tommaso Guidi; Guercino, "Squint-eyed,
originally Giovanni Francesco Barbieri; Il Bronzino, "Sun
burnt," Agnolo di Cosimo di Manano; and, flatly, Il So
doma, "the Pederast," who was Giovanni Antonio Bazzi.

The French sculptor Clodion was Claude Michel. I hav
no idea why he changed, but the modern French painte
Julius Pincas made an anagram of his last name and becam
Jules Pascin.

The Russian columnist Melor Sturna devised his first nam
as an acronym of Marx, Engels, Lenin, October Revolu
tion.

It cheers me to remember that there is a Swiss psychiatris
named Dr. Dotti (he is Audrey Hepburn's husband, by th
way); and that Yreka, CA, is the home of the palindromi
Yreka Bakery. Mention of Dr. Dotti reminds me that on th
authority of Elizabeth Longford's superb *Victoria R.I.*, th
hygienically pure obstetrical staff attending the Queen a
the birth of Prince Leopold (1853) included Dr. Snow, Mrs
Innocent, and Mrs. Lilly; and, finally, that her daughte
Princess Victoria's wet nurse came from Cowes.

Names For Pets

The Bishop of Litchfield drives his own horses, "Pride" and "Prejudice." He says people may consider it a terrible thing for a bishop to be drawn hither and thither by these passions, but then it is assuredly a fine thing to have them well under control.

AUGUSTUS J. C. HARE, *The Story of My Life*

Nick Ludington had a Manx cat named Bellevue, and General Bob Richardson had a pet skunk named Chanel, and William Beckford, the eccentric author of *Vathek*, had a dog named Viscount Fartleberry.

True, we don't know the name of Paul Revere's horse, but in Landseer's famous painting *Dignity and Impudence*, the bloodhound was Grafton and the Scottish terrier was Scratch. The RCA-Victor fox terrier that is listening to His Master's Voice is named Nipper.

A tenacious mastiff was named Pharaoh because of Exodus 5:1: "The Lord said to Moses: Go unto Pharaoh and say . . . : Let my people go."

A springer spaniel with chronic eczema also took his name, Moreover, from the Bible, on the authority of St. Luke 16:21: "moreover the dogs . . . licked his sores."

Dorothy Parker called her canary Onan, because (see Genesis 38:9) he spilled his seed on the ground. She also had a Scottie named Alexander Woollcott Parker, of whom Woollcott wrote, "He reversed the customary behavior of a

namesake by christening *me*—three times, as I recall—in
single automobile ride."

George Washington's pack of foxhounds included Lady
Vulcan, Searcher, Rover, Sweetlips, Truelove, Chaunter
Dabster, Countess, Musick, Mopsy, Old Harry, Statley, Ju
piter, Venus, Singer, Jowler, Forrister and Ringwood. Ther
was a Ringwood in John Peel's pack:

> Yes, I ken John Peel and Ruby too,
> Ranter and Ringwood, Bellman and True. . . .

According to Godfrey Smith in the *Sunday Times* of Lon
don, if you happen to own a pet aardvark, there is only on
possible name for it—"Emilion"—in tribute, of course, t
the line in Al Jolson's song: "Aardvark Emilion miles fo
one of your smiles, my Mammy!"

I once knew a cat named Waldo Fostoria.

"I just bought a pet zebra."
"What are you going to name him?"
"Spot."

"Hee-Haw"

Miss Eleanor Cross of Baltimore had a cat named Magnifi-cat.

Nature Notes

The eggshells of all members of the hawk family are green inside.

Alone among mammals, man and the Dalmation coach hound have uric acid in their urine. Alone among birds, the ostrich yields leather.

British spiders eat yearly a weight of insects equal to that of the human population of Great Britain.

W. S. BRISTOWE

(A spider is not an insect, but an arachnid.)

Only adult male crickets are able to chirp; if you count the number of their chirps in fifteen seconds and add 40, the result will be the temperature within one degree Fahrenheit.

Every year, around the Feast of the Virgin (August 15th), thousands of harmless cat snakes (so called from their manner of stalking lizards) appear on Corfu, crawl about for a few days, then disappear for another year.

In doves the red spot at the base of the parents' bill guides the youngsters' aim to the right spot for regurgitated food. Doves lay two eggs, always of the same sex. They are the only birds that suck up water, as a horse does, instead of taking a bill full and letting it trickle down the throat.

Doves symbolize peace, and hawks symbolize war? Dr. S. Dillon Ripley, a trained ornithologist (and former Secretary of the Smithsonian), has this to say: "Hawks are sensible, full of wisdom, and not ferocious; whereas doves are cruel, insensate, and far more bloodthirsty."

Of the 18 different mammals that man has domesticated, the pig stands without rival as the most intelligent of the larger kinds, the dog as the smartest of the smaller. In rating all animals by intelligence, the pig ranks just below the apes. Wild pigs can open locks with their snouts. In competition with rats in a multiple-choice maze with nine doors, no rat required fewer than 200 trials, whereas no pig required more than 40.

CLIFFORD S. POPE

In the early nineteenth century, two brothers living on the edge of the New Forest, in England, domesticated a wild Berkshire sow and taught her to hunt birds. Slut, as they named her, because of her muddy flanks, could catch the scent from forty yards, and when the bird flushed and was shot, she would retrieve it. She attained the majestic weight of 700 pounds and died at the age of about ten.

According to Barrow's *Travels in Southern Africa*, hyenas have been trained to hunt and retrieve small antelopes; and according to *History of Field Sports, Part I*, sparrows have been trained to catch butterflies on the wing and retrieve them.

The song of the willow warbler, according to a correspondent in *Country Life*:

Sip, sip, sip, see!
Tee, tew, wee, tew!
Witty, witty, wee-wee, weetaw!

A mule will always lift its tail before it brays.

A sassafras shrub may have leaves of three totally different shapes on the same twig.

What is generally thought of as the peacock's tail—the feathers that make up that beautiful fan with "eyes"—is not a tail at all, but the upper tail *coverts*. The actual tail feathers are short and drab. Among the many, many legends about peacocks is one that says their flesh never decays but "continues as it were embalmed in spices."

During the Great War parrots were kept in the Eiffel Tower to give warning of approaching planes. Their hearing was so acute that they could detect a plane long before human spotters.

In the newborn infant, the navel divides the body into two equal parts.

MATILA GHYKA, The Geometry of Art and Life

The elephant's period of gestation, eighteen months, was thought the longest of all mammals' until the recent discovery that the armadillo's may run to 20 months.

A zebra is a white animal with black stripes.

You can lead a cow upstairs, but not down.

If you touch a turkey's nest or a guinea's, the hen will abandon it; so, to move the eggs, you should use a long-handled spoon—a silver one, purists say.

Usually only male birds sing; females do so rarely.

When twin calves are of different sexes, both will be sterile.

I think I was the first to go into print with the fact that swallows fly in front of golfers, picking up disturbed insects.

DJM, a nature writer in the *Times* of London

Ostriches kick *forward*; the male's kick is powerful enough to be lethal.

. . . the marvelous old mulberry tree [in the Deanery at Canterbury] to preserve the life of which a bullock was actually killed that the tree might derive renewed youth from its blood.

AUGUSTUS J. C. HARE, *The Story of My Life*

Dogs are color-blind.

Atop the canyon I saw two of the little black deer whose hind feet leave no scent. It's an odd quirk of nature, in the way of self-protection. Their front feet (or hooves) leave scent like all other deer. But in moments of danger, these frisky little fellows run with such precision that the hoofmarks are superimposed, staving off predators—lynxes, cougars, wolves, even bears in a surly humor.

ROBERT LEWIS TAYLOR, *A Roaring in the Wind*

The opposite of Lipizzan stallions, which are dark brown when they are foaled and later turn white, Imperial Black swans (and turkey buzzards) are white when they are hatched and later turn brown.

The scientific name of the common European grosbeak is *Coccothraustes coccothraustes coccothraustes*.

Russians have an almost pathological dislike for yellow tulips; nobody seems to know why.

In 1929, the *London Illustrated News* carried a photograph of a fish that had recently been caught off the coast of Zanzibar. The natural markings on one side of its tail spelled out *La-ilaha-illa Allah* (Arabic for "There is no god but Allah"), and on the other side, *Shan Allah* ("God's work"). And in 1806, a panic terror of the end of the world seized the good people of Leeds [England] and its neighborhood.

A hen, in a village close by, laid eggs on which were inscribed the words "Christ is coming."

CHARLES MACKAY, *Extraordinary Popular Delusions and the Madness of Crowds*

Queen Anne abhorred the smell of roses, and the sight of a lily threw the historian Scaliger into convulsions.

Guinea pigs fight when empty milk bottles are clicked together.

"The Notebooks of James Thurber"

Bamboo is technically a grass, and the banana tree is an herb. The fig is the only tree from which we eat the flower.

To grow prize onions, you should bury clippings from horses' hooves deep down, near the tips of the roots.

[Baroness Blixen (Isak Dinesen):] "Did you know that a lion never looks directly at you? He looks *past* you in order to spare you embarrassment."

FREDERIC PROKOSCH, *Voices*

All breeds of dogs have a normal temperature of 100° to 102°, with the exception of the Mexican hairless, whose temperature runs to 104°.

In parts of China men carry tame quail in cold weather, to warm their hands.

As well as their eight legs, octopuses also have two kidneys and three hearts. So do squids.

Only the male bamboo is suitable for making the shaft of the spear used in the sport of pigsticking.

During World War I, a patriotic poultry breeder managed to cross a Rhode Island Red with a White Leghorn and an Andalusian Blue, to produce a chicken that was red, white, and blue. He called the bird Americana.

"Say, Pollen, do you know anything about birds?"
"Yes, sir."
"How are you on linnets? Do you happen to know what sort of noise they make?"
"Yes, sir. The rough song of the linnet is 'Tolic-gow-gow, tolic-joey-fair, tolic-hickey-gee, tolic-equay-quake, tuc-tuc-whizzie, tuc-tuc-joey, equay-quake-a-weet, tuc-tuc-wheet'."

P. G. WODEHOUSE, *Summer Moonshine*

The cathedral at Metz boasts that in one of its towers, there is the dried body of a real dragon, "Groggy."

The male mosquito is a gentleman . . . while madame his spouse is a whining, peevish, venomous virago, that goes about seeking whose nerves she may unstring and whose blood she may devour. Strange to say, not among mosquitoes only, but among ticks, fleas, chiggers, and the whole legion of blood-thirsty, stinging flies and midges, it is only the female that attacks man and beast. Stranger still, the mosquito is not only a bloodsucker but an incorrigible wine-bibber as well—it will get hopelessly fuddled on any sweet wine, such as port, or on sugared spirits, while of gin it is inordinately fond.

MEL WHITE, *Virginia Wildlife*

Armadillos can catch malaria and therefore are useful for laboratory studies of the disease.

Nicknames, Pseudonyms, Sobriquets and Noms de Plume

The Rev. Charles James Grimble, Muriel A. Schwartz, Charles Augustus Conybeare, Helen B. Trundlett, J. A. D. Spence—all these were pseudonyms that T. S. Eliot used when he was editing (and contributing to) the correspondence page of *The Egoist*.

Mary Ann Evans wrote as "George Eliot"; Aurore Dupin as "George Sand"; Mrs. P. M.T. Craigie as "John Oliver Hobbes," and Charlotte, Emily and Anne Brontë as "Currer, Ellis and Acton Bell." Did any man ever take a woman's name as his *nom de plume*? (I except T. S. Eliot, above).

We are accustomed to the adoption of pseudonyms by writers, actors, artists, pop singers, prize fighters, and members of religious orders, but it is surprising to learn that a famous architect also used a pseudonym: Le Corbusier's real name was Charles Édouard Jeanneret.

"Three Hands" was the nickname bestowed on T—— H——by a disheveled maiden who could find no other explanation for having been so overwhelmed by his boudoir blitzkrieg.

Melba's real name was Nellie Mitchell. She took her sta name from Melbourne, Australia, which was near her birt place.

England's most famous landscape gardener, "Capabilit Brown (1715–83), was so nicknamed because he used say that a site "had capabilities of improvement." His re first name was Lancelot.

The American Confidence Man, by David W. Maurer, lis the professional names of some of them: the Hashhou Kid, Hoosier Harry, Farmer Brown, Johnny on the Spo Cheerful Charlie, the Harmony Kid, Count Lustig, Plu Drucker, the High-Assed Kid, 102nd Street George, Lin house Chappie, the Narrow Gauge Kid, Wildfire Joh Omaha Blackie and the Indiana Wonder.

Brooklynites were once called "Trolley Dodgers"; citize of Lisbon are still called "Lettuce Eaters"; and those Brussels, "Chicken Guzzlers." One of the strangest su sobriquets is the one "enjoyed" by citizens of Maline Mechelin, in Belgium. It traces back to a night more than century ago, when a visitor from Antwerp, seeing the mo shining full and red on the tower of St. Rombaut's Cath dral, began to shout, "People of Malines, wake up! Yo tower is on fire!" The whole city turned out and ran to t tower, carrying buckets of water, and they have be known as "Moon Extinguishers" ever since.

W. C. Fields had such a terror of being caught broke th whenever he visited a city for the first time, he hurried open a bank account. Unhappily he often failed to keep record of the bank's name, the pseudonym he chose f himself, and the amount of the deposit; but it has been es mated that there were some 700 of these accounts, totali more than $1 million. The twenty-three pseudonyms th survive include Aristotle Hoop, Sneed Hearn, Cholmond ley Frampton-Blythe and Figley E. Whitesides.

Noise

As [John] Leach got older . . . his extreme sensitiveness to noise became more acute, and when at last he became subject to slight attacks of *angina pectoris*, his descriptions of his sufferings from street noises were painful to hear. My last talk with Leach was on a certain Tuesday, at a dinner party . . . in Queen Anne Street. His constant talk during dinner was of the annoyances he was subjected to by organs, bands, barking of dogs, cock-crowing, etc. "Rather," he said, "than endure the torment that I suffer all day long, I would prefer to go to the grave where there is no noise." He died on the following Saturday from a severe attack of *angina pectoris*, and in the following week he was in the grave "where there is no noise."

W. P. FRITH, *My Autobiography and Reminiscences*

Schopenhauer was driven almost mad on Saturdays, by the noise of cattlemen cracking their whips over their oxen. The imperturbable Max Beerbohm would jump uncontrollably at sudden noises. The Italian poet and Nobel prizewinner, Salvatore Quasimodo, was tormented by the noise of rug beating in Naples—so much so that he wrote to the mayor, begging that it be done at different hours on different days. Dumas Père could not tolerate the slightest sound in the house when he was writing. Emperor Augustus had a mortal dread of the sound of thunder and, at the approach of the smallest storm clouds, would retire to a soundproof vault which he had had built for this purpose.

Noise infuriated [Edward Lear]. In Rome . . . he was reduced to distraction by an odious operatic neighbor, "a vile beastly rottenheaded foolbegotten pernicious priggish, screaming, tearing, roaring, perplexing, splitmecrackkle crackmecringle, insane ass of a woman . . . practising howling downstairs with a brute of a singing master so horribly that my head is nearly off." In Switzerland, the children at his hotel, "forty ill-conducted little beasts," caused him to curse the species; while in Paris he complained of the cats . . . "four hundred and seventy-three . . . making an infernal row in the garden close to my window."

PETER QUENNELL

Gibbon tells somewhere (I can't find the reference) about the Roman emperor who awoke in Alexandria one morning with such a hangover that the cheerful noise of the streets was an agony. To quiet it, he ordered out his legions, who slew 5,000 people.

[Thomas Carlyle said:] "That which the world torments me in most is the awful confusion of noice. It is the devil's own infernal din all the blessed day long, confounding God's works and his creatures—a truly awfu' hell-like combination, and the warst of a' is a railway whistle, like the screech of ten thousand cats, and ivery cat of them all as big as a cathedral."

AUGUSTUS J. C. HARE, *The Story of My Life*

I have always heard that if one stayed long enough in Port Said the whole world would pass before him. . . . The whole world passes before you if you have a room on the 5th floor of the Muehlebach Hotel [in Kansas City]. . . . The din that a small, corrupt city can raise between the hours of 1 P.M. and 10 A.M. is indescribable, certainly by me. Rudyard Kipling could probably do it, or James T. Farrell. Every bus, streetcar, vendor, hawker, factory whistle, blows and clangs at full blast. Every streetcar has at least one flat wheel, and every bus one flat tire. It was as close to a madhouse as I ever expect to get, present company excepted. The concerted din . . . can make a 5-grain Seconal hang its head in shame. Having tried everything else, I finally crawled under the bed and rooted for the atomic bomb.

Letter from GROUCHO MARX to Goodman Ace

The loudest noise in recorded history was the explosion in August 1883 of Krakatoa volcano in Sunda Strait, between Java and Sumatra. It was heard clearly in Bangkok, 1,413 miles away, and in Ceylon, 2,058 miles away, and faintly on Rodrigues Island, nearly 3,000 miles away.

The next loudest noise was probably the explosion of the munitions ship *Mont Blanc* in the harbor of Halifax, Nova Scotia, in December 1917. It was heard at North Cape Breton, 225 miles away.

The Rebel Yell was "a high-pitched holler . . . a mixture of fright, pent-up nervousness, exhaustion, hatred and pure deviltry . . . fierce, fiendish, savage, demoralizing . . . a maniacal maelstrom of sound . . . rasping, shrieking, blood curdling. . . ."

A composite description from several sources

Vienna requires garbage cans to have rubber lids.

The noisiest country I have ever visited is Portugal. An English lady who has lived there for seventeen years told me, "The Portuguese are impervious to noise." I believe it. Commercial and social transactions are conducted full-throated. Radios run at full blast, and the tile floors and bare plaster walls in restaurants, shops, and houses bounce the sounds back and forth. The hordes of stray dogs that infest every community bark all night long, without protest from the citizens. One morning in the public square at Albufeira, I saw a hollow-eyed American tourist kick a dozing dog. "Wake up, you S.O.B.!" he said, "*You* can sleep tonight!"

Old Age

What a cunning and insidious thing, in its approach, is old age! How it steals upon you in the night! How carefully it looks you over before it strikes! Confronting you like a cunning antagonist, it fences cautiously until it sees where your guard is weak; it toys and feels with its point, for some opening where, in careless youth, you removed the shield of health and did not replace it; and then, when the spot is found, with quick and unerring thrust, it pinks you.

JOHN SERGEANT WISE, *Diomed*

When we grow old, and our own spirits decay, it reanimates one to have a number of living creatures about one, and to be much with them.

JOHN WILMOT, *Earl of Rochester*

John O'Hara: "It's a sure sign you're over the hill when the man at the filling station stops calling you 'Mac' and starts calling you 'Doc.'"

I'd add to that: And when the barber asks, "Trim the ears and nostrils?" And when you see a bishop or a butler younger than yourself. "Over the hill" reminds me of a line from one of Jack White's recitatives at his Club Eighteen: "Over duh hill to duh poorhouse. . . . Goin' to duh poorhouse wasn't tough enough—dey hadda put a hill in front of it."

Of young men die many; of old men escape not any.

JOHN RAY

One of its penalties is having to carry so much lumber when you travel: pills and salves, extra eyeglasses, canes and mufflers, hot-water bottles.

A lady who was born in 1792 and died in 1882 told me that one of the advantages of living to be very old was that one came to see that things which had seemed to be disaster were really blessings. "For instance," she said, "when Princess Charlotte [King George IV's daughter and heir] died [in 1817], the whole nation was plunged into grief. And now we have lived to know that she was a rantipole [Webster "A wild, romping young person: also, a termagant"], and that it was the greatest mercy she never came to the throne."

GEORGE W. E. RUSSELL, *An Onlooker's Note-book*

Shallow. Jesu, Jesu, the mad dayes that I have spent! And to see how many of my olde acquaintance are dead!

Silence. Wee shall all follow, coosin.

Shal. Certaine, 'tis certaine, very sure: death, as the Psalmist saith, is certaine to all, all shall die. . . . Is old Dooble of your towne living yet?

Sil. Dead, sir.

Shal. Jesu, Jesu, dead! a drew a good bow: and dead! John a Gaunt loved him well, and betted much money on his head. . . . And is old Dooble dead?

SHAKESPEARE, *2 Henry IV*

I used to have four supple members and one stiff one. Now I have four stiff ones and one supple one.

DUC DE MORNY

Madame de Rothschild, dying: "No, Doctor, I don't want to grow young again. I just want to keep on growing old."

Where the Devil cannot go, he sends an old woman.

German proverb

After a certain distance, every step we take in life we find the ice growing thinner below our feet, and all around us and behind us we see our contemporaries going through.

ROBERT LOUIS STEVENSON, *Virginibus Puerisque*

One's graces—thank God!—aren't the prey of age, as one's sight and sinew are.

ADMIRAL S.

Memorial services are the cocktail parties of the geriatric set.

SIR RALPH RICHARDSON

Put cotton in your ears and pebbles in your shoes. Pull on rubber gloves. Smear Vaseline over your glasses, and there you have it: instant old age.

MALCOLM COWLEY, *The View from 80*

An old, old woman who was asked how she contrived to get through her day, replied, "Well, you see, I coughs a bit, and I scolds a bit, and I prays a bit, and it all helps to pass the time."

FREDERICK LOCKER-LAMPSON, *My Confidences*

Kate said to an old man, "What are you so low about, my man?"

"Why," he said, "what wi' faith, and gas, and balloons, and steam ingines a-booming and a-fizzling through t' warld, and what wi' t' arth a-going round once in 24 hours, I'm fairly mizzled and stagnated."

AUGUSTUS J.C. HARE, *My Life*

[Lady Waterford:] "I think Captain Williams must be no longer young, because he is so very careful about his dress, and that is always a sign of a man's growing old, isn't it?"

IB.

Si jeunesse savait!
Si vieillesse pouvait!

You know you're getting old when the candles cost more than the cake.

BOB HOPE

You know you're growing old when everything hurts. And what doesn't hurt doesn't work.

HY GARDNER

A theater usher came to Ethel Barrymore's dressing room and said, "There's a lady out here who wants to tell you hello. She says she went to school with you."

Miss Barrymore said, "Wheel her in!"

If you live to be one hundred, you've got it made. Very few people die past that age.

GEORGE BURNS

A florist, to Finis Farr, who was ordering flowers for an elderly lady: "Ah, yes, dear old Mrs. G——. She's peeping through the westward window, is she not?"

Satchel Paige, the late great black pitcher, formulated these six rules for staying young:

1. Avoid fried meats, which angry up the blood.
2. If your stomach disputes you, lie down and pacify it with cool thoughts.
3. Keep the juices flowing by jangling around gently as you move.
4. Go very lightly on the vices, such as carrying on in society.
5. Avoid running at all times.
6. Don't look back. Something may be gaining on you.

Onomatopoetics

O lente, lente currite noctis equi.

MARLOWE, *Dr. Faustus*

The moan of doves in immemorial elms,
And murmuring of innumerable bees.

TENNYSON, "The Princess"

Dosen't thou 'ear my 'erse's legs, as they canters awaäy?
Proputty, proputty, proputty—that's what I 'ears 'em saäy.

IB., "Northern Farmer. New Style"

The thunder and surge and the baffled roar
[of waves] which shatter, and pass in foam and spume.

JAMES BRANCH CABELL, "Sea Scapes"

Lone poplars, sisters of fallen Phaëthon,
 Quivering innumerate inconsolable leaves.

W. C. IRWIN, "The Objects of the Summer Scene"

Strong gongs groaning as the guns boom far,
Don John of Austria is going to the war.

G. K. CHESTERTON, "Lepanto"

Les sanglots longs
Des violons
 De l'automne

Blessent mon coeur
D'une langueur
Monotone.

VERLAINE,
"Chanson d'Automne"

"How does the water
Come down at Ladore?" . . .
Rattling and battling
And shaking and quaking,
And pouring and roaring. . . .
And falling and brawling and sprawling
And sounding and bounding and rounding,
And grumbling and rumbling and tumbling. . . .
And thumping and plumping and bumping and jumping,
And dashing and flashing and splashing and clashing,
All at once and all o'er, with a mighty uproar—
And this way the water comes down at Ladore.

ROBERT SOUTHEY, Selections from
"The Cataract of Ladore"

(Do you know where Ladore is, by the way? In Cumberland, northwestern England.)

The clock ticks spoke with castanet clicks.

CARL SANDBURG

The silken sad uncertain rustling of each purple curtain.

EDGAR ALLAN POE, The Raven"

The tintinnabulation that so musically wells
From the bells, bells, bells, bells,
Bells, bells, bells—
From the jingling and the tinkling of the bells

IB., "The Bells"

. . . The quick sharp scratch
and blue spurt of a lighted match.

ROBERT BROWNING, *"Meeting at Night"*

The limousine crawled crackling down the pebbled drive.

F. SCOTT FITZGERALD, "Love in the Night."

The Papacy

Pope Silverius (536–37) was the son of a pope, Homisdas (514–23); and Pope John XI (931–35 or 36) was the son of Pope Sergius III (904–11).

Adrian IV (1154–59) was the only English pope; his lay name was Nicholas Breakspear.

Pope Leo X (1513–21): "Since God has been pleased to give us the Papacy, let us enjoy it."

Pope Urban VIII (1623–44) had all the nightingales in the Vatican gardens killed; their warbling disturbed his sleep.

Pius IX (1846–78) was probably the most beloved person in Italy when he was elected Pope. A few months later he was driving through Rome and happened to glance up at a window where a nurse was holding a child. She dropped it; it was killed, and right there began the rumors that he had the Evil Eye. Presently it was whispered that Italy had been winning the Austrian campaign until he blessed the cause and thereby cursed it. They say that the day he blessed the column being raised to the Virgin in the Piazza di Spagna, a workman fell to his death from the scaffolding. He said mass at the Basilica di Sant'Agnese, and the floor collapsed. To "prove" that these stories were true, the Italians pointed out that it was during Pius IX's pontificate that the papacy lost its temporal power.

Pope Leo XIII (1878–1903), was also believed to have the Evil Eye; he was blamed for the assassination of King Umberto in 1900. When Leo was a cardinal, he was one of the earliest stockholders in the company that controls the Monte Carlo casino, the Société des Bains de Mer et Cercle des Étrangers. His was the longest pontificate; twenty-five years and three months. Pope Stephen II's was the shortest: three days (752).

The irrigation system that Pope Pius XI (1922–39) installed in the Vatican gardens included a number of secret gadgets by which he could drench unsuspecting visitors (especially the new cardinals) when he took them for a stroll.

Pope John XXIII (1958–63): "It often happens that I wake up at night and begin to think about a serious problem and decide I must tell the Pope about it. Then I wake up completely and remember that I *am* the Pope."

Vatican Palace is the largest residence in the world, and until recently the largest *building*; it covers thirteen acres and contains 11,000 rooms and 200 staircases. Vatican City has more telephones per capita than any other city in the world.

A legend says that when a pope dies and presents himself at the Pearly Gates, St. Peter steps aside and lets him admit himself with his own key. One pope, a winebibber, fumbled around ineffectually until St. Peter came to his rescue and let him in. He had been trying to use the key to the Vatican cellars.

Paris

I well remember leaving London on a morning in January 1868 in a fog so thick that the footman had to lead the horses all the way to Charing Cross Station. Ten hours later I found myself in a fairy city of clean white stone houses, literally blazing with light. I had never imagined such a beautiful, attractive place. Paris certainly deserved the title of "la Ville Lumière."

LORD FREDERIC HAMILTON,
The Days Before Yesterday

The oldest bridge in Paris is the Pont Neuf, "New Bridge."

The Salvation Army hostel, in the XIII arrondissement, was designed by Le Corbusier and is hung with paintings by Fernand Léger.

Irkutsk once liked to call itself the "Paris of Siberia." There is no record that Paris ever called itself the "Irkutsk of France."

Those eight statues of buxom women that stand on pedestals around the Place de la Concorde represent eight major French cities. Victor Hugo's mistress posed for Strasbourg, and Lille's pedestal is the entrance to a boat tour of the Paris sewers.

Is there another city on earth with shops and restaurants so endearingly named? Sniff this bouquet of titles: A toy shop: The Blue Dwarf. A general store: A Bit of Everything. An antiques shop: The Bad Taste. Children's clothing: Blue,

White, Pink. A restaurant: A Feather in the Wind. A department store: In Springtime. A bistro: The Why Not?

You take Hammacher Schlemmer; I'll take Blue, White, Pink.

When God becomes bored in heaven, he opens the window to see what is happening on the boulevards of Paris.

HEINRICH HEINE

The popular public swimming pool, the Piscine Deligny, in the Seine near the Pont de la Concorde, was built from the timbers of the huge funeral car that bore Napoleon's ashes from the Arc de Triomphe to the Invalides, in December 1840. The upper part of the Pont de la Concorde itself was built with stones from the ruins of the Bastille.

The bistro that once occupied a corner on the Rue du Repos, immediately across from Père Lachaise Cemetery, is gone now, but I like to remember its cynical name: Mieux Ici Qu'en Face ("Better Here Than Facing Us").

The Man in the Iron Mask is buried in St. Paul Cemetery, not far from the Bastille, as "Marchiali." His true identity is one of the best kept secrets in history. I don't know even the reason for the pseudonym "Marchiali."

The headquarters of the Syndicat des Concierges is located, most appropriately, on the Rue du Dragon.

A Paris lawyer, Maître P——, specializes in defending vandals charged with desecrating the Tomb of the Unknown Soldier.

If you stand somewhere along the axis of the Champs-Élysees on the afternoon of any May 5 and face the Arc de Triomphe, you will see it frame the setting sun, beautifully and precisely. It is a nice coincidence that May 5 is the anniversary of the death of Napoleon, who had the arch built.

When the Bazar de Charité was held in Paris in 1897, the cream of society, the *gratin*, attended. Fashionable ladies presided at the stalls, and fashionable gentlemen bought their wares. Suddenly fire broke out. In moments, the flimsy tents and booths, decorated with bunting and paper garlands, became an inferno. The sole exit was quickly choked; many tried to escape being burned alive, only to be trampled to death or suffocated. The search for the dead continued all night by the light of lanterns. The victims—127 of them, including the Duchesse d'Alençon, sister of Empress Elisabeth of Austria-Hungary—were laid out in the Palais de l'Industrie, nearby. Some say that only 5 of the bodies were men's; others that none was. But it is certain that next day not one man in all Paris admitted having been to the bazaar.

Personal Descriptions

She was as flat-chested as an ambidextrous Amazon.

She walked as if her knees were strapped together, and she had rockers on her feet.

She was built like a boy arrow.

E. M. ASHCRAFT, III

He was forty inches from tit to tit and smelled like eight wet rams.

R. S. RUSH, of a friend of his, an all-American fullback

He had a profile like a flight of steps.

A corpulent voluptuary.

KIPLING, of King Edward VII

He looked like Death taken seasick.

SWINBURNE

[Elizabeth Barrett Browning's] physique was peculiar: curls like the pendent ears of a water-spaniel, and poor little hands—so thin that when she welcomed you she gave you something like the foot of a young bird.

FREDERICK LOCKER-LAMPSON, *My Confidences*

Of the nineteenth-century murderer John Williams: "The oiliness and snaky insinuation of his demeanour counteracted the repulsiveness of his ghastly face, and amongst inexperienced young women won for him a very favourable reception."

THOMAS DE QUINCEY

She could hold six kitchen matches on her eyelashes.

He can't whisper, he can't tiptoe, and he won't hurry.

MARY GRAY, of her husband, Dixie

We could never get a definite *yes* or *no* from him. We thought of him as "the Man with the Diagonal Nod."

M. W. BUFFINGTON

When [a certain Chinese actor] bade me adieu, his hand felt like a bundle of fingernails.

MARY ANDERSON, *A Few Memories*

. . . one from whose soft, silky greys and mauves comes the faintest perfume of roses as she moves, and in whose laces and lawn nestle unaudacious pearls.

LADY NORAH BENTINCK,
My Wanderings and Memories

[Thomas] Carlyle—weird and grim with his long coat and tall wizard-befitting hat.

AUGUSTUS J. C. HARE, *The Story of My Life*

Mr. Wooster looks like a church-brass incarnated, and turns up his eyes when he speaks to you, till you see nothing but the whites.

IB.

He had the widest, blackest an' best-groomed an' longest beard I've ever seen off a yak.

KIN HUBBARD, *Abe Martin*

. . . Gurdjieff, that strange and mysterious man who attracted so many unusual people to his college at Fontainbleu [*sic*]. . . . He used to say he could smell a person five miles away. Asleep, his body could be lifted by two men; awake, a dozen of us could not budge him. To this day, I carry a scar on my left wrist, the result of his hand being laid casually over mine. The pressure, inert weight, was so great it burst the tissues and skin. I have seen Gurdjieff crash through benches and chairs that would surely have supported the weight of an elephant.

Etheric Notes of Gerald Light

She had a wart on the left side of her chin, with one long black hair growing out of it. When she sneezed, it cracked like a whip; and if she caught cold, she flogged her cheek raw.

PINKY THOMPSON

He had so many gold teeth than when he smiled, it looked as if a pipe organ were being unveiled.

The greatest of the [Susquehanna Indian] *werowances* [chiefs] was one the calfe of whose leg was 3 quarters of a yard about and all the rest of his limbes so answerable to that proportion, that he seemed the goodliest man that ever we beheld. His haire, the one side was long, the other shorn close with a ridge over his crown like a cock's combe.

CAPTAIN JOHN SMITH,
The Generall Historie of Virginia . . .

[Giacomo] Leopardi, the Italian poet [1798–1837], was undersized, slightly deformed, near-sighted, prematurely bald, nervous and weak.

EDGAR SALTUS, "The Genesis of Disenchantment"

[Of a man with a fearful hangover:] He was shining like a bad lobster in a dark cellar. He looked like you could take a ladle and stir him around.

H. S. R.

[The artist J. M. W.] Turner...was small and had "a lobster-red face, twinkling, staring grey eyes," wore "an ill-cut brown coat," "turned up boots, large fluffy hat," and carried round a huge umbrella, beneath which he was accustomed to sketch on a diminutive piece of paper "held almost level with his waist."

PETER QUENNELL, *Customs and Characters*

When the brilliant but ferocious Gen. Alfred M. Gruenther was Supreme Allied Commander in Europe (1953–56), his staff liked to boast that he was the only man "who could get *expression* (usually furious impatience) into an electric buzzer, and could plough furrows in the glass top of a desk with his fingernails."

Thomas Chatterton's father could put his clenched fist into his mouth.

Jules Renard said that Tristan Bernard's mouth was "like a frail pink boat in the black river of his beard."

CORNELIA OTIS SKINNER,
Elegant Wits and Grand Horizontals

Slim and graceful as a Siamese cat, [Count Robert de Montesquieu] was absurdly handsome, with dark, wavy hair and a silky moustache beneath a proud Roman nose....There was something definitely artificial about his skin, and Léon Daudet...describes him as being "ageless, as though varnished for eternity, every line of his brow cleverly ironed out."

IB.

A thin dirty fellow with stringy hair and the look of an onanist.

Paris and the Arts, 1851–1896, from the *Goncourt Journal*

[St. Francis of Assisi, at twenty-seven:] Round head, low forehead, black eyes without malice, a delicate straight nose, little, almost pointed ears, a vehement sweet voice, white teeth, even and close together, thin lips, spare beard, delicate neck, short arms, long fingers and fingernails, thin legs, little feet and little or no flesh on his bones.

GLENWAY WESCOTT,
A Calendar of Saints for Unbelievers

Coleridge looks like an archangel a little damaged.

CHARLES LAMB

[W. H.] Auden's face looks like a wedding cake that was left out in the rain.

STEPHEN SPENDER

[Wilde's] pale hands were enormous and ugly, and he waved them about while talking, a cigarette between his fingers, making prelatical gestures: and though his eyes were fine, bright-grey, they were rather prominent and had a steady stare in them which contrasted disconcertingly with the dreamy, word-caressing inflections of his delightful voice.

DESMOND MACCARTHY, "Oscar Wilde"

[The Confederate troops arrived at Winchester, on Christmas Day 1861], and as they marched through town next morning, Private Peterkin had his first sight of a man with heavy dark whiskers and hair, his trousers thrust into his boot tops, and wearing a long blue overcoat, standing in the crowd on the sidewalk. He had a faded gray cap pulled down so low over his face that little of it could be seen except a pair of piercing dark eyes. It was Stonewall Jackson.

ROBERT EDWARD LEE STRIDER,
The Life and Work of George William Peterkin

Mrs. Digby Vallence was tall and spare, with a small face, big eyes, and a large mouth. Digby was fond of saying that his wife's face was geometrically impossible. The parts were greater than the whole. She was a very amiable, intelligent woman, who played Schumann with a weak wrist, and was noted for her cooking recipes.

JOHN OLIVER HOBBES, *The Sinner's Comedy*

Prodigies

Theodore Hook (1788–1874) wrote and produced a successful comedy at the Drury Lane Theatre when he was sixteen.

William Henry West Betty (1791–1874) made his stage debut at eleven and soon was playing such difficult Shakespearean roles that he was known as "the Young Roscius." The House of Commons once adjourned to see his "Hamlet."

Beethoven (1770–1827) played in public at eight.

Richard Strauss (1864–1949) wrote a polka and a song at six.

Mozart (1756–91) composed minuets before he was four.

John Stuart Mill (1806–73) began learning Greek at three.

William Crotch (1775–1847) of Norwich, England, played "God Save the King" on the organ, treble, and bass at two years and three months.

Christian Heinecken, born in Lübeck, Germany, in 1721, began to speak at the age of ten months and had memorized the principal events of the Pentateuch at one year. At two he had mastered sacred history. At three, "he was intimately acquainted with history and geography," according to the *Encyclopaedia Britannica*, "besides being able to speak French and Latin." In his fourth year, he began the study of religion and church history. But before he was five, he died.

The Professional Point of View

Mr. Clarkson, the wig-maker, on being asked his opinion of a great Shakespearean production, declared it to be superb. "You couldn't see a join," said he, meaning thereby that the line where the wigs of the actors joined their foreheads was invisible.

EDWARD H. SOTHERN, *My Remembrances*

There is a good picture of my grandfather, in his naval uniform, at Aldenham; it is by a well-known painter, Gilbert Charles Stuart. Old Boswell, my grandfather's shipmate and body-servant, is said to have pronounced this portrait a success, "particklar the buttons."

FREDERICK LOCKER-LAMPSON, *My Confidences*

When old Green, the frame-maker, had finished the frame for Holman Hunt's *The Finding of the Saviour in the Temple*, Hunt went to see it and told him it was quite satisfactory. "Ah," said Green, "but you'll see the picture will set it off amazingly."

HENRY HOLIDAY, *Reminiscences of My Life*

Prophets Without Honor

There is no likelihood man can ever tap the power of the atom.

ROBERT MILLIKEN, Nobel Prize in physics, 1923

While theoretically and technically television may be feasible, commercially and financially I consider it an impossibility, a development of which we need waste little time dreaming.

LEE DE FOREST, 1926

"What, Sir? Would you make a ship sail against the wind and currents by lighting a bonfire under her deck? I pray you excuse me. I have no time to listen to such nonsense."

NAPOLEON to Robert Fulton

In the opinion of competent experts it is idle to look for a commercial future for the flying machine. There is, and always will be, a limit to its carrying capacity which will prohibit its employment for passenger or freight purposes in a wholesale or general way. Some . . . will argue that because a machine will carry two people, another may be constructed that will carry a dozen, but those who make this contention do not understand the theory of weight sustentation in the air; or that the greater the load the greater must be the lifting power (motors and plane surface), and that there is a limit to these . . . beyond which the aviator cannot go.

W. J. JACKMAN, M.E., AND THOS. H. RUSSELL, A.M., M.E., Flying Machines: Construction and Operation, 1910

Everything that can be invented has been invented.

CHARLES H. DUELL,
Director of U.S. Patent Office, 1899

We must not be misled to our own detriment to assume that the untried machine can displace the proved and tried horse.

MAJ. GEN. JOHN H. HERR, 1938

That is the biggest fool thing we have ever done. . . . The [atomic] bomb will never go off, and I speak as an expert in explosives.

ADM. WILLIAM LEAHY
to President Truman, early 1945

The energy produced by the breaking down of the atom is a very poor kind of thing. Anyone who expects a source of power from the retransformation of these atoms is talking moonshine.

ERNEST RUTHERFORD

There is no hope for the fanciful idea of reaching the moon, because of insurmountable barriers to escaping the earth's gravity.

DR. F. R. MOULTON,
astronomer, University of Chicago, 1932

Wilbur Wright has made the statement that in his opinion the use of the aeroplane for dropping bombs or explosives into a hostile army is impracticable, as the machine must rise 1,000 or 1,500 ft. above the ground to escape shell fire. At that height accuracy would be impossible in dropping explosives when moving at 40 or 50 miles an hour.

Popular Mechanics, July 1909

Rail travel at high speeds is not possible because passengers, unable to breathe, would die of asphyxia.

DR. DIONYSIUS LARDNER (1793–1859)

It is not at all bad being a businessman. There is a spirit of trust and cooperation here. . . . If businessmen were not trusting of each other and could not set their great projects going on credit, the country would collapse tomorrow and be no better off than Saudi Arabia.

WALKER PERCY, *The Moviegoer*, 1960

Puns

[Daniel Francois Auber, the composer of *Fra Diavolo, Le Domino Noir*, etc., was having tea with Prince Metternich, a chain-smoker.]

Metternich said to Auber, "*Vous me permettez?*", wanting to put his ashes in Auber's tea-saucer. Auber said, "*Certainement, mais j'aime mieux monter que descendre.*" In other words, *J'aime mieux mon thé que des cendres.* (I like my tea better than ashes.)

LILLIE DE HEGERMANN-LINDENCRONE,
In the Courts of Memory

Invitations, the sincerest form of flattery.

A. J. A. SYMONS

Thomas Moore described Charles Lamb as "full of villainous and abortive puns, which he miscarries of every minute."

Quelle est la différence entre Paris, l'ours blanc, Amundsen et l'Impératrice Catherine?

Paris est métropole;
l'ours blanc est maître au pole;
Amundsen aime être au pole;
l'Impératrice Catherine aimait trop Paul.

I remember Miss Fortescue explaining that the Greeks had a custom of carving speeches on their seats. It seemed there was a term for these which she had forgotten. She appealed

to [William Schwenck] Gilbert: "What were they called?"
"*Arrière-pensées*, I expect," replied Gilbert.

JEROME K. JEROME, *My Life and Times*

Motto of the Beefsteak Club, London:

> If it were done when 'tis done, then 'twere well
> It were done quickly. . . .
>
> *Macbeth*

"Why stand ye here all the day idle?" said my father to Mr. Ben Wolf, the writer, and to Mrs. F. A. Harris, who was bidding good-by to her husband.

Said Dr. Harris, "We are the scribes and the F. A. Harrises."

EDWARD H. SOTHERN, *My Remembrances*

When Bill Spackman saw the tablet near our house that marks the "outer line of Richmond's defenses, 1862–65," he observed: "Ah, the line of Lee's resistance!"

Non sum qualis eram sub regno bony Sinatra.

JAMES THURBER

Put-Downs

The Duke of Buccleuch met an Esterhazy prince at the Court of St. James's and boasted that he had 5,000 sheep on his estate in Scotland.

"How odd!", the prince replied. "That is exactly the number of shepherds I have."

ANDREW SINCLAIR, *The Last of the Best*

The Earl of Sandwich: "I am convinced, Mr. Wilkes, that you will die either of a pox or on the gallows."

John Wilkes: "That depends, my Lord, on whether I embrace your mistress or your principles."

A French lady, to an American lady trying to converse in French: "How wise of you not to attempt the French accent!"

[Samuel] Rogers [the poet, 1763–1855] met Lord Dudley at one of the foreign watering-places, and began in his vain way, "What a terrible thing it is how one's face pursues one, and that one can never get away from one's own identity! Now I sat by a lady the other night, and she began . . . 'I feel sure you must be Mr. Rogers.'"

"And *were* you?" said Lord Dudley.

AUGUSTUS J. C. HARE, *The Story of My Life*

"I didn't come here to be insulted!"
"No? Where do you usually go?"

Palace Theater, c. 1920

Dorothy Parker, to an aggressively objectionable person: "When you get home, throw your mother a bone."

Charles Lamb, to a friend at the card table: "Martin, if dirt were trumps, what hands you would hold!"

This is not strictly a put-down, because no one who ever knew the kindly, gentle Moss Hart would even *wish* to put him down. He and his wife, Kitty Carlisle, bought a handsome house in Bucks County, Pa., and Hart immediately set about landscaping it. When the job was done, the Harts invited Wolcott Gibbs, *The New Yorker*'s drama critic, down for a weekend, and Hart showed him around. "I brought in that clump of beeches from over *there*," he said, "and put them *here*. Then we put the willows in to balance them. Now, the forsythia. . . ."

When he had given the complete tour, he asked Gibbs, "What do you think of it?"

Gibbs said, "It just goes to show what God could do if he had your money."

Judge Hunter Marshall was taking his ease and his noontime toddy at the Westmoreland Club, in Richmond. Finding the room somewhat stuffy, he told one of the club servants, "Nathan, open that window, please."

The club bore, Major W——, materialized from nowhere. "Judge," he said, hitching up a chair, "that reminds me of a story. It seems—"

"Nathan!" the Judge cried, "Nathan, close that window!"

Sophie Arnould, a singer at the Paris Opéra in the late eighteenth century, was as famous for her wits as for her beauty. Ernest Newman tells of the time when a rival actress received a magnificent diamond rivière from her lover, and a friend remarked to Sophie what a pity it was that its length made it fall too low on the lady's person. Sophie said, "The river is returning to its source."

Richard Brinsley Sheridan, to a Mr. Courtenay, a fellow member of Parliament: "The honourable member is indebted to his memory for his jests, and for his facts to his imagination."

[Rome, 1886.] Baroness K. inveigled Franz Liszt into taking tea with her, and when he accepted, she invited a lot of friends, holding out hopes that Liszt would play. She pushed the piano into the middle of the room—no one could have possibly failed to see it. Liszt arrived and saw the situation at a glance. After several people had been presented to him, he said to the hostess:

"*Où est votre piano, chère madame?*", and looked all about for it, though it was within an inch of his nose.

"Oh, Monseigneur! Would you, really?... *Here* is the piano!"

"Ah," said Liszt, "true! I wanted to put my hat on it."

LILLIE DE HEGGERMANN-LINDENCRONE,
The Sunny Side of Diplomatic Life

Tourist in Vermont:

"Make any difference which road I take to White River?"

Native: "Not to me it don't."

ALLEN R. FOLEY, *What the Old Timer Said*

Actor:

"I've never been better! In the last act yesterday, I had the audience glued to their seats."

Oliver Herford: "How clever of you to think of it!"

An Irishman well-known in London was Frank Murphy, a member of Parliament for Cork, pleasant and witty, considerably bumptious too. When he visited Cork during vacation, his great delight was to astonish natives by his London ways and manners. At a large dinner party at the house of an old gentleman, immediately after dinner he lit a cigar and began to smoke, a custom unheard of in Ireland then. His old host was equal to the occasion: "Indeed, then it is kind of you, Frank, for your old grandmother always took a shough [draw] of the pipe after pratees [potatoes]."

W. R. LE FANU, *Seventy Years of Irish Life*

A resident of Kerry, who dearly loved a lord, lost no opportunity of talking of his great acquaintances. At a dinner party where there were several Roman Catholics, during a conversation on the subject of fasting, this gentleman said, "It is very strange how little Catholics in the higher ranks mind the fast days. I was dining at the Duke of Norfolk's on a fast day, three weeks ago, and there wasn't a bit of fish at dinner."

"I suppose," said Pat Costello, "they had eaten it all in the dining room?"

IB.

Said Uriah [Heep] with his sickliest smile, "But *I* am not changed, Miss Trotwood."

"Well, sir," returned my aunt, "to tell you the truth, I think you are pretty constant to the promise of your youth, if that's any satisfaction to you."

CHARLES DICKENS, *David Copperfield*

George Bernard Shaw found on sale in a secondhand bookshop a book he had presented to a friend, inscribed "With the compliments of GBS." He bought it and sent it back to his friend, additionally inscribed, "With renewed compliments."

When Alexander Woollcott was appearing in his first play in New York there was no question in his mind . . . that people thought and talked of little else. That was why Charlie [MacArthur] would every now and then give Woollcott a ring and invite him to dinner. "If you have nothing better to do tonight." It never failed to set Woollcott on fire.

The Letters of Nunnally Johnson

n Lord Northcliffe's afternoon walk home from his office t the *Daily Mail*, he used to drop in at the august Athen-eum Club to use its lavatory. After some months of this, an ttendant ventured to ask him if he were a member. North-liffe was—or pretended to be—astonished: "Good Lord! s this place a club, *too*?"

n 1871 when London was once more full of French aristo-ratic refugees [from the Franco-Prussian War] the Duc de 3roglie . . . observed to Lady William Russell that he had ever believed till now that the English were a nation of hopkeepers . . . whereupon she replied that she had always elieved until now that the French were a nation of sol-iers.

T. WEMYSS REID, *Life and Letters of Richard Monckton Milnes, Lord Houghton*

'he pride which often accompanies exalted birth is curi-usly susceptible to the charms of insolence; one of the reatest pleasures of the brainless but haughty lies in being umbled.

PETER QUENNELL, "George Bryan Brummell"

)ld Lord Leicester, watching a cricket match at Lord's, ropped his umbrella. The Duke of Portland, sitting near im, picked it up and handed it back, saying, "I'm Port-and." There was no response, so he repeated, "I'm Port-and." Lord Leicester grunted, "I never said you weren't," nd returned his attention to the match.

Told by the VISCOUNT DE L'ISLE, V. C., K. G.

ack White, the star comedian at the famous Club 18 (West 'ifty-second Street, New York), to a loud, persistent eckler: "Why do you heckle me? For all you know, I'm 'our father."

The scene was a luncheon party at the Broughams'; the appointed time, 1:30. Till 1:45 we waited for Lady Cunard; and at two o'clock she arrived, full of apologies—she had been buying a chandelier. Old Lord Brougham, a handsome patriarch with silver hair, looked straight in front of himself and said in a pensive tone: "I once knew a man who bought a chandelier *after* luncheon."

EDWARD MARSH, *A Number of People*

When an actress asked Father Mugnier if it was a sin to look at herself naked in a mirror, he gave a quick glance at her overfulsome figure and solemnly replied, "No, madame, it's an error."

CORNELIA OTIS SKINNER,
Elegant Wits and Grand Horizontals

A silly chatterbox countess once told [Lucien Guitry], with a giggle, "You know, I simply talk the way I think!" to which the actor's comment was "Yes, but more often."

IB.

Alaska to Texas: "If you don't stop bragging, I'll split up two for one, and then you'll be the *third* largest state!"

John [Wilkes] toasted George III ostentatiously in front of . . . the Prince of Wales, and, asked whence dated this anxiety for the King's longevity, replied, "Since I had the honour of Your Royal Highness's acquaintance."

OLGA VENN, "John Wilkes"

The Prince suffered a similar put-down, though neither intentional nor so brutal, when he was sitting for to the eccentric sculptor, Joseph Nollekens. King George III was then convalescing from a long illness, and Nollekens asked the Prince, "How's your father?"

"He is much better, thank you."

"Splendid!" Nollekens said. "I would be sad if he was to die. We shall never have another king like him!"

While out walking in Portsmouth, the Prince Regent saw Jack Towers across the way, and called out, "Hullo, Towers! I hear you are the greatest blackguard in the place." Towers answered, bowing, "I hope Your Royal Highness has not come here to take away my reputation."

LEONARD RUSSELL, Introduction to *English Wits*

[Dissatisfied client:] "Do you call that a good piece of art?"
[Whistler:] "Do you call yourself a good piece of Nature?"

WYNDHAM LEWIS, "Whistler"

[Boring young man:] "I was born between twelve and one on the first of January. Isn't that strange?"
[John Wilkes:] "Not at all. You could only have been conceived on the first of April."

IB.

Betsy Patterson Bonaparte, visiting Mrs. Tabb of White Marsh, in Gloucester County, Va., remarked that she had not expected to find as much society "in these backwoods" and that next time she came, she would bring her best clothes.

Mrs. Tabb said firmly, "There will be no next time, Betsy."

Told by MRS. PHILLIP HAMILTON

The dramatic critic of the *Police Gazette*, a pink paper that was read only in barbershops . . . had written something offensive about my father [actor Maurice Barrymore] and the next time they met he said, "Did you see what I wrote about you, Barrymore?"

And father said, "No, I shave myself."

ETHEL BARRYMORE, *Memories*

One of the Hollywood moguls was screaming at my brother Jack and shaking his finger in his face. Jack said, "Put that finger down! I remember when it had a thimble on it."

IB.

. . . the stagehand said, just as [the great black entertainer Bert] Williams came off stage and passed him, "He's a good nigger. Knows his place."

And Williams mumbled, "Yes. A good nigger. Knows his place. Going there now. Dressing room ONE!"

IB.

Barbra Streisand stops at a gas station. "Your face looks familiar," says the attendant. "Haven't I seen you someplace before?"

Barbra: "Maybe at the neighborhood theater."

Attendant: "Maybe. Where do you usually sit?"

TRIBUNE MEDIA SERVICES, INC.

Quotations Quiz

(ANSWERS ON NEXT PAGE)

Quote correctly and give the source:

1. To gild the lily.
2. Pride goes before a fall.
3. Money is the root of all evil.
4. A fool and his money are soon parted.
5. Fold their tents, like the Arabs,
   And as silently steal away.
6. Care killed the cat.
7. Comparisons are odious.
8. All is not gold that glitters.
9. Familiarity breeds contempt.
10. The even tenor of their way.
11. A little knowledge is a dangerous thing.
12. Speed the parting guest.
13. The man that hath no music in his soul.
14. Fresh fields and pastures new.
15. A thing of beauty and a joy forever.
16. Alas! poor Yorick. I knew him well.
17. Why don't you come up and see me sometime?
18. Home is the hunter.
19. Under a spreading chestnut tree.
20. The light that never was on land or sea.
21. It takes a heap o' livin' t' make a house a home.
22. "God bless us all!" cried Tiny Tim.
23. How doth the little busy bee
    Improve each shining hour!
24. Say it ain't so, Joe!

QUOTATIONS QUIZ *(Answers)*

1. To gild refined gold, to paint the lily.

SHAKESPEARE, *King John*

2. Pride goeth before destruction, and an haughty spirit before a fall.

PROVERBS

3. The love of money is the root of all evil.

1 Timothy

4. A fool and his words are soon parted; a man of genius and his money.

attributed to WILLIAM SHENSTONE

5. *This is correct.*

LONGFELLOW

6. Care killed a cat.

SHAKESPEARE, *Much Ado About Nothing*

7. Comparisons are odorous.

IB.

8. Nor all that glistens, gold.

THOMAS GRAY

9. Familiarity begets boldness.

SHACKERLEY MARMION

10. The noiseless tenor of their way.

THOMAS GRAY

11. A little learning is a dangerous thing.

POPE

12. Speed the going guest.

IB.

13. No music in himself.

SHAKESPEARE, *The Merchant of Venice*

14. Fresh woods and pastures new.

MILTON

15. Is a joy forever.

KEATS

16. I knew him, Horatio.

Hamlet

17. Why don't you come up sometime and see me?

MAE WEST, *She Done Him Wrong*

18. Home is the sailor, home from the sea,
And the hunter home from the hill.

R. L. STEVENSON

19. *This is correct.*

LONGFELLOW

20. The light that never was on sea or land.

WORDSWORTH

21. It takes a heap o' livin' in a house t' make it home.

EDGAR A. GUEST, "Home"

22. "God bless us every one!" said Tiny Tim, the last of all.

DICKENS, *A Christmas Carol*

23. *This is correct.*

ISAAC WATTS

24. It ain't true, is it, Joe?

Young baseball fan to "Shoeless Joe" Jackson, implicated in the "Black Sox Scandal."

Religion

Note on theolatry: Egypt worshiped the goat as Mendes; the hawk, as Sobk-Re; the bull, as Apis; the ibis, as Thoth; the beetle, as Khepri; the cat, as Bubastis; the falcon, as Horus; the cow, as Hathor; the snake, as Merseger; the ram, as Amon; the jackal, as Anubis; the hippopotamus, as Opet; and the vulture, as Mut. The Scandinavians worshiped the Midgard Snake and the Fenris Wolf. The Cimbri worshiped a brazen bull; the Israelites, a golden calf; the Hairy Ainus, a bear; the Aztecs, a serpent, Quetzalcoatl; and the Hindus, an elephant, Ganesha. Alone among animals, the dog, which man has never worshiped, worships him.

Note on the company of saints:

When St. Clement, the fourth Bishop of Rome, fled to escape prosecution, he put a layer of wool on his saddle. The heat and sweat of his body, and the chafing motion and pressure, made it into the first felt, so he is the patron saint of hatters.

Episcopalianism is a nice, light little religion, suitable for summer.

C. D. S.

The God of the Calvinists is the Devil with "God" written on his forehead.

ARCHBISHOP WHATELY

More pleasing in the sight of the Almighty . . . , and more like what Jesus Christ intended man to become, is an honest Turk with 6 wives, or a Jew working hard to feed his little old clo' babbies, than those muttering, miserable, mutton-hating, man-avoiding, misogynic, morose & merriment-marring, monotoning, many-mule-making, mocking, mournful, minced-fish & marmalade masticating Monx [of Mount Athos, Greece].

VIVIEN NOAKES, *Edward Lear*

St. Pyro, a chronic alcoholic, drowned himself while drunk.

DR. EDWARD S. GIFFORD, JR., *The Evil Eye*

When Chandos Pole was Master of the Cattistock Hounds in Dorset, he entertained the Bishop of the Diocese. I asked him how he had got on. Chandy said, "Oh, he's a very good fellow indeed. I had a charming dinner and evening with him, but when I asked him if he would have some kümmel with his coffee, he said, 'What *is* kümmel?'" Chandy remarked, "Just fancy making a man a bishop who doesn't know what kümmel is."

THE DUKE OF PORTLAND,
Memories of Racing and Hunting

Savonarola preached throughout Lent in 1492 on the text of Noah's Ark, giving each day a different interpretation of the ten planks.

'Tis said by men of deep research,
He's a good dog who goes to church.
I hold him as good, every bit,
Who stays at home and minds the spit;
For tho' good dogs to church may go,
The *going there* don't make 'em so.

FREDERICK LOCKER-LAMPSON,
My Confidences

The reason the bishops' benches in the House of Lords are the only ones in the chamber which have arms to them is to stop drunken bishops rolling off the seats and onto the floor.

JOSEPH GRIMOND, M. P.

Guillaume Parel (1489–1565), a Swiss Billy Graham, refused to cut short his long sermons even when the women in his congregation routed him from the pulpit and dragged him down the aisle by his beard.

When the Bishop, visiting, saw champagne glasses on the table, he began his blessing "O bountiful Jehovah," but when he saw only a water glass, he began "Even for these, the least of thy mercies—"

AUGUSTUS J. C. HARE

The official name of the English Church in Leningrad is "British Factory in Leningrad," and the official name of Westminster Abbey is "the Collegiate Church of St. Peter in Westminster."

The Russian cab-drivers, the *Skopetzi* [in Jassy, Romania], belonged to a special sect of Old Believers whose males castrated themselves after the birth of their first child.

MATILA GHYKA, *The World Mine Oyster*

[Haughty,] like that Archbishop of Canterbury who could be approached only on gilt-edged paper.

G. W. E. RUSSELL, *Collections and Recollections*

Beaverbrook's old Catholic friend, Tim Healy, once told him: "Our old monks kept a separate pen to write the name of God and did so always on their knees."

PETER HOWARD, *Beaverbrook*

St. Cunegund, who out of humility abandoned all care of her body. St. Opportune, who never touched water nor washed her bed save with her tears. [St. Catharine of Sweden wept for four hours every day.] St. Silvie, who never cleaned her face. St. Radegund, who never changed her hair-skirt and slept on ashes. [St. John Joseph of the Cross went for sixty-four years without changing his clothes.] St. Luce's body was so transparent that through his bosom dirtiness could be detected in his heart.

J. K. HUYSMANS, *Down There*

When [Muhammad] had to go to the privy, he took off his signet ring; then he stepped into the privy with his left foot first, saying: O God, I take refuge with Thee from all uncleanness. He stepped out with the right foot, saying: Thy Pardon!

ERIC SCHROEDER, *Muhammad's People*

When the coffin which contained the remains of Stephen [the first martyr of the Christian faith] was shown to the light, the earth trembled, and an odour, such as that of paradise, was smelt, which instantly cured the various diseases of seventy-three of the assistants.

GIBBON, *The History of the Decline and Fall of the Roman Empire*

The baptismal name of St. Francis of Assisi was Giovanni.

The Rt. Rev. Richard Hooker Wilmer, Bishop of Alabama, is the only bishop ever consecrated in the Protestant Episcopal Church of the Confederate States of America.

Dr. Cumming, the minister [of the Scottish Presbyterian Church in London], was principally known for always prophesying the imminent end of the world. He had been unfortunate in some of his predictions, the dates having slipped by uneventfully, but he finally fixed on a date in 1867 for the Great Catastrophe. His influence with his flock rather diminished when it was found that he had renewed the lease of his house for twenty-one years, only two months before.

LORD FREDERIC HAMILTON, *The Days before Yesterday*

The Bishop of Bermuda's see includes Newfoundland.

From La Baumette [Rabelais] was sent to the Cordeliers or Gray Friars at Fontenay-le-Comte, "*où l'on faisait voeu d'ignorance plus encore que de religion*" ["Where one took a vow of ignorance rather than of religion"]. So deeply were they imbued with the belief in the vanity of human knowledge, that they regarded a desire to acquire it, if not as a proof, at all events a strong presumption, of heresy.

J. LEWIS MAY, "Introduction to the Works of Rabelais"

Muhammadans believe that ten animals have been admitted to paradise, but only these ten: Jonah's whale, Solomon's ant, Balkis's lapwing, Abraham's ram, Saleh's camel, Balaam's ass, Moses's ox, the Seven Sleepers' dog Kratim, Muhammad's ass, and Noah's dove.

On Dean Lockyer's return to England from Rome, King George I jocularly asked him if he had "succeeded in converting the Pope."

Lockyer answered, "No, Your Majesty. His Holiness has most excellent Church preferment and a most desirable bishopric, and I had nothing better to offer him."

St. John Raynuce [fourteenth century] was a saint of whom nothing is known. His remains were discovered in the sixteenth century by a fanatic.

GLENWAY WESTCOTT,
A Calendar of Saints for Unbelievers

The number of angels abroad in the world—since the quantity according to Church doctrine was fixed at Creation, the aggregate must be fairly constant. An exact figure—301,855,722—was arrived at by 14th-century cabalists.

GUSTAV DAVIDSON, *A Dictionary of Angels*

St. Germain raised a disciple from the dead, who told him, "He was well and all things were to him soft and sweet," and St. Germain permitted him to stay dead.

E. V. LUCAS, *A Wanderer in Paris*

No, I don't go to church. I'm a sort of flying buttress—I support the church from outside.

JOHN SANDS

The Clergy would have us believe them against our own reason, as the woman would have had her husband against his own eyes, when he took her with another man, which she stoutly denied: what, will you believe your own eyes before your own sweet wife?

Table Talk of John Selden

After St. Ambrose (ob. 397) was elected bishop of Milan, he felt obliged to become a Catholic.

Crosses come in at least twenty different shapes, including the potent, the pommée, the avellan and the moline.

There was a Dr. Taylor who used to worship the heathen gods—Mars and Mercury and the rest. One day at Oxford, in the presence of my father and one of the professors, he took his little silver images of the gods out of his pocket and began to pray to them and burn incense. . . . The same Dr. Taylor was afterward arrested for sacrificing a bullock to Neptune in a back-parlor in London.

AUGUSTUS J. C. HARE, *The Story of My Life*

I know men, and I tell you that Jesus Christ was not a man.

NAPOLEON to Beauterne, on St. Helena

Rome

St. Peter's is the largest church in the world, 2⅓ times the size of Notre Dame.

The famous Spanish Steps are owned by France, which leases them to Italy for an annual fee of one lira (now about 0.0007 cent).

Native Romans speak of the Tiber not by name, but as "River."

The five chapels of Santa Maria della Concezione, on the Via Veneto, are friezed, garlanded, panoplied, and festooned with human bones. Even the chandeliers are grisly arrangements of tibias and femurs and ulnas and skulls. I once heard an American wife ask her husband, "Whose are they?"

"Tourists," he said glumly. "Picked clean."

Actually they are the bones of some 5,000 Capuchin friars who died there between 1528 and 1870. Santa Maria's most famous friar was one Pacifico, known to Rome of the 1840s as *Il Mago*, "the Wizard," because of his ability to predict winning numbers in the lottery. The word flashed around town, and so many gamblers began packing Santa Maria's services that the regular congregation complained to Pope Gregory XVI, who had the Wizard banished. To the crowd of grieving gamblers who came to see him off, he gave his farewell blessing—and *five* winners! (I wish I knew where *his* bones are!)

There are four Roman sounds that will echo forever in my memory's ear: the early-morning rattle of jalousies being drawn up; the *whop!-whop!-whop!* of rugs being beaten; the itinerant broom seller's wailing "*Sco-pa-a-a-a-aro!*"; and the sidewalk glazier's bubbling flute, like a shepherd boy's. Hearing any one of them would instantly carry me back to Via Antonio Gramsci, where I lived for a happy winter.

Mr. Hamilton asked what he thought of Rome and Naples. "Wal," said Sandy, "I just think that if naething happens to Rome and Naples, Sodom and Gomorrah were very unjustly dealt with."

AUGUSTUS J. C. HARE, *The Story of My Life*

What image does the word "Colosseum" bring to your mind's eye? Here's what it brought to mine: A huge, hot, dusty, roaring arena, with lions gnawing on meek Christians, while gladiators mangle one another, and Nero lounges on rose leaves, turning down his thumb from time to time: "Let him die!"

I say "brought," not "brings," because I read up on the Colosseum and then visited it, and everything I'd "known" about it proved to be utterly wrong.

First, Nero never even heard of it; its cornerstone wasn't laid until ten years after his death. Second, few modern historians believe that many, or even *any*, Christians were martyred there. Nor, third, do they believe that thumbs-down meant death; they agree with Juvenal, an eyewitness, that thumbs-*up* was the signal for death, thumbs-*down* for clemency. Lastly, neither Nero, gladiators, early Christians, nor Juvenal ever spoke of the "Colosseum"; to them it was always the "Amphitheatrum Flavium." The name "Colosseum" was not attached until the eighth century.

Surprised?

Rome has two separate smells: in season, roasting chestnuts, and all year round, the pervasive Romaroma of stale urine. When I took Corey Ford to see the former royal palace, the Quirinal, he sniffed twice, then shook his head. "Misprint," he said.

If you go to the Borghese Gallery, you can't miss Canova's statue of Pauline Bonaparte, nude. Touch her cool little marble belly and make a wish. It is *sure* to be granted!

The part of my guidebook devoted to the Borghese has this item: "1st Room—LXIV. The Rape of Cassandra, a relief." I sent a photocopy of it to *The New Yorker*, which printed it with the comment, "Just give information, please."

Until the eighteenth century, when some authority foolishly decided to weed the Colosseum, it was a compact botanical garden, sheltering some 420 species of plants. The seeds were brought there probably in the fodder that accompanied the wild animals imported for the gladiatorial "games," though Ouida romantically preferred to believe that they "had lodged in the sandals of the legions as they marched home from Palmyra and Babylon." Caper plants are still abundant in the crevices, the only place I ever saw capers that weren't in a jar.

One of the daily sights on the Via Veneto thirty years ago was the Emperor of Byzantium. Don't snicker! The Italian courts recognized his name and his right to ennoble you, if he wished. Ladies curtsied to the sad little fellow when they met. He was better known as the Marchese Antonio de Curtis and best known as Totò, the famous clown.

Royalty

King Henry VII's queen, Elizabeth, is the original of the depiction of the four queens in a deck of playing cards.

Princess Margaret, who was born at Glamis Castle, Scotland (August 21, 1930), is the first member of the British Royal Family to be born north of the border since Charles I (1600).

George II of Greece was not King of Greece, but King of the Hellenes, being of non-Greek (i.e., Danish) descent. Similarly, Baudouin is not King of Belgium, but King of the Belgians, being of Saxe-Coburg-Gotha descent.

The Duc de Morny (1811–1865) said of himself, "I am a very complicated person. I am the son of a queen, the brother of an emperor, and the son-in-law of an emperor, and all are illegitimate." (He was the son of Queen Hortense by Count Flahaut, and thus an illegitimate brother of Napoleon III; and his wife was the daughter of Emperor Nicholas I of Russia.)

When the brother of Czar Nicholas II came from St. Petersburg to Cannes, railway traffic all over Europe slowed down; Grand Duke Michael had a weak heart and insisted that his private train go no faster than 30 mph.

LEONARD SLATER, *Aly*

At the famous ball given by Charles the Mad, that is, Charles VI of France (1368–1482), the King and his courtiers dressed as savages, with feathers gummed to their skins. Out of high spirits they threw blazing torches at one another and set the feathers and other costumes on fire, and six guests were burned to death.

MATILA GHYKA, *The Strange Life of Objects*

William Duke of Gloucester, nephew of King George III, and affectionately called "Silly Billy," greeted with enthusiasm a naval officer of great distinction who attended the levee on his return from foreign service. "We haven't seen you at court for a long time."

"Well, no, sir; since I was here last I have been nearly to the North Pole."

"By G——, with your red face, you look as if you had been to the *South* Pole!"

GEORGE W. E. RUSSELL, *An Onlooker's Note-book*

Everyone likes flattery; and when you come to royalty, you should lay it on with a trowel.

BENJAMIN DISRAELI

When they dip their pens of gold into their veins of azure—ah, the boredom, and, hush, the vulgarity!

LOGAN PEARSALL SMITH

Go in front of royalty, but never *pass* in front of them.

Attributed to Princess Mary, the Princess Royal

Edward VII was famous for his tact. For example, his three herds of cattle at Sandringham were deliberately chosen to represent the three divisions of his kingdom: shorthorns for England; Highlanders for Scotland; Dexter-Kerrys for Ireland.

The first time a shah of Persia visited a British monarch, at Buckingham Palace in 1873, he sacrificed a sheep in one of the guest rooms. Queen Victoria was "intensely annoyed."

When George III learned of the accession of Emperor Peter III of Russia in 1762, he observed, "There are now nine of us in Europe, the third of our respective names." The nine were himself and Peter, Charles III of Spain, Augustus III of Poland, Frederick III of Prussia, Charles Emmanuel III of Sardinia, Mustapha III of Turkey, Francis III of Modena, and Frederick III of Saxe-Gotha.

The Duke of Windsor had eight successive titles: Prince Edward of York, Prince Edward of Cornwall and York, Prince Edward of Wales, Duke of Cornwall, Prince of Wales, King Edward VIII, Prince Edward of Windsor, and finally Duke of Windsor.

When Queen Elizabeth II visited New Zealand in 1953, the Maoris gave her the title "The Rare White Heron of the Single Flight."

When the Shah [Reza Pahlevi] travels, the dogs are killed in a village where he spends the night.

JOHN GUNTHER, *Inside Asia*

Queen Victoria's father, the Duke of Kent, once had tea with Martha Washington.

[King Edward VII's] handshake and his bow, most of his gestures and many of his words and acts had become invested with a very wide range of calculated and subtly differentiated degrees of significance, and his manner of raising his hat, for example, or the intonation of his voice, were adjusted by a sixth sense, which had become second nature, to the stature of the person whom he was addressing and to the occasion and place of meeting.

PHILIP MAGNUS, *King Edward the Seventh*

Louis XIV had six different ways of tipping his hat, each showing a different degree of cordiality.

Henry III of England [1207–72] slept with raw veal chops on his cheeks, and his hands covered with pomade, and tied to the tops of the bed by silk cords, so that they would be white in the morning.

Ferdinand VII of Spain (ob. 1833) liked to embroider petticoats for statues of the Virgin.

Maximilian II of Bavaria never smiled, from boyhood to the day of his death, at fifty-three, in 1864. His son, Ludwig II, closed his eyes when he conversed and regarded Marie Antoinette as the reincarnation of the Virgin Mary. His dining table was an elevator; it could be lowered into the kitchen and the dishes changed there, so that he would never have to see his servants. Ludwig's brother Otto barked like a dog and did not take off his boots for eight weeks.

King Christian VII of Denmark (1749–1808), an epileptic homosexual, was tiny and feeble and cruel. He once leapfrogged over the Neapolitan Ambassador and did not hesitate to toss boiling tea into the face of his courtiers.

King João I of Portugal (1357–1433) had a room in Sintra Palace painted with 132 chattering magpies, as a rebuke to the gossipy ladies of his court.

Ojin-Tenno of Japan was born an emperor, in 201, and reigned until his death 109 years later.

Being royal has many painful drawbacks.

DAISY ASHFORD, *The Young Visiters*

The sons of George III all of them swore lustily; but I think the Duke of Cumberland was the only scion of royalty who habitually swore when conversing with the Archbishop of Canterbury.

FREDERICK LOCKER-LAMPSON, *My Confidences*

"I hate all boets and bainters!"

KING GEORGE I of England

Emperor Franz Josef I of Austria was also a king four times over (of Hungary, Bohemia, Dalmatia, and Lodomeria), three times a duke (of Bukovina, Upper Silesia, and Lower Silesia), and marquess of Moravia.

Carlo II of Parma (1799–1883) had a notable collection of pornographic watches.

I spent the morning with Philip of Hesse and we talked of how most of the royalties of Europe have a cockney accent acquired from English nannies.

Chips: The Diaries of Sir Henry Channon

Among the titles and sobriquets of Sulayman the Magnificent, an Ottoman sultan of the sixteenth century, were the following: Allah's Deputy on Earth, Lord of the Lords of This World, Possessor of Men's Necks, Emperor of the East and West, King of the Believers and Unbelievers, Seal of Victory, Prince and Lord of the Most Happy Constellations, Refuge of All the People in the Whole World, Chief of All the Ends of the World, Shadow of the Almighty Dispensing Quiet on Earth, and Commander of All Kings Which Can Be Subject to Command. Whereas the twentieth-century King Prajadhipok of Siam was merely Arbiter of the Ebb and Flow of the Tides, Brother of the Moon, Half-Brother of the Sun, and Possessor of the Four-and-Twenty Umbrellas.

Philip II of Spain (1527–98), whom many historians consider a cowardly tyrant, had the largest heart ever recorded in medical history.

King Farouk of Egypt to the Prince of Wales, later King Edward VIII: "Someday there will be only five kings: the kings of spades, hearts, diamonds, and clubs and the King of England."

King Leopold of the Belgians wore a black wig, a feather boa, rouge, and shoes with soles three inches thick.

Queen Mary [the wife of King George V] was never heard to laugh in public.

ANNE EDWARDS, *Matriarch*

King George VI is unique among English sovereigns of recent centuries in that the exact time of his death is unknown (he died in his sleep). It follows that the exact time of Queen Elizabeth II's accession also is unknown.

IB.

The Sexes

The superiority of the male over the female sex is clearly implied from the fact that when we overcome a difficulty we say we Master it, but if we fail in our aim we Miss it.

PROFESSOR AUGUSTUS DE MORGAN

Overheard years ago "under the clock" at the Biltmore Hotel, New York, when it was a favorite tryst for preppies and collegians: Impatient swain, to the date who finally shows up: "I've looked at that clock so often I know every number on it by heart!"

Never make the Big Pitch until the second date.

International swordsman

If her eyes don't quite track, it's a sign of a sure kill.

IB.

Chaucer interpreted gaps between her teeth as another sign of ready availability. Cf. his lusty Wife of Bath: "Gat-toothed I was, and that became me well."

It is observed that the red-haired of both sexes are more libidinous and mischievous than the rest, whom yet they much excel in strength and activity.

SWIFT, *Gulliver's Travels*

To Carthage then I came, where a cauldron of unholy loves sang all about mine ears.

ST. AUGUSTINE, *Confessions*

But I, wretched, most wretched, in the very commencement of my early youth, had begged chastity of Thee, and said, "Give chastity and continency, only not yet." For I feared lest Thou should hear me soon, and cure me of the disease of concupiscence, which I wished to have satisfied, rather than extinguished.

IB.

One special form of contact, which consists of mutual approximation of the mucous membranes of the lips in a kiss, has received a sexual value among the civilized nations, though the parts of the body do not belong to the sexual apparatus and merely form the entrance to the digestive tract.

FREUD, *The Sexual Aberrations*

So many beautiful women and so little time!

JOHN BARRYMORE

A tender, sensitive young female tells how she felt when first he kissed her—like a tub of roses swimming in honey, cologne, nutmeg and blackberries.

S. S. COX, *Why We Laugh*

Love is a funny thing, shaped like a lizard,
Run down your heartstrings and tickle your gizzard.

Blues song from New Orleans

Col. Milton Buffington, to a notorious libertine: "Is it true that the day after you moved into your new apartment, a family of self-respecting minks moved out of the one next door?"

I have always heard that one of the first outward signs of the decadence of a race is that the girls grow taller, while the men get shorter.

LORD FREDERIC HAMILTON,
The Vanished Pomps of Yesterday

King Adolphus Frederick of Sweden (1710–71) declared that the foundation of true love is pity; practicing this preachment, he had two one-eyed mistresses, two one-legged, two one-armed, and one with no arms at all.

Miss A. F., of a notorious pouncer: "He missed his calling. He should have been a proofreader for the Braille Press."

A lisping lass is good to kiss.

'Tis safe taking a shive [i.e., a slice] of a cut loaf.

More 'longs to marriage than four bare legs in a bed.

The difference is wide
That the sheets will not decide.

A dog's nose and a maid's knees are always cold.

Free of her lips, free of her hips.

All from JOHN RAY,
A Compleat Collection of English Proverbs

Princess Helena Victoria recalled how on one occasion, just before they went in to dinner, Grandmamma [Queen Victoria], having concluded that her granddaughter's dress was too low, pointed with her fan and said, "A little rose in front, dear child, because of the footmen."

H. R. H. PRINCESS ALICE, Countess of Athlone,
For My Grandchildren

A distinguished Civil Servant of mature years and head of a Department was arrested with a prostitute in flagrant delight on an open bench in Hyde Park late at night, in icy weather. Repeating each phrase, Winston Churchill said slowly—"Why, it makes me proud to be an Englishman!"

Sunday Times of London book review

Men, some to business, some to pleasure take;
But every woman is at heart a rake.

POPE, *Moral Essays*

Christopher Gibbs and his wife Peggy have grown to look exactly like one another—an infallible indication of a happy marriage.

JAMES LEES-MILNE, *Prophesying Peace*

Anatole France said of his wife: "She is a rare woman. She has an opinion about everything, but never gives it."

In 1922 a woman in Sheffield, England, confessed to sixty-one marriages in five years.

My uncle Gagnon said, "You're ugly, but your ugliness won't be held against you, because you've got expression. Your mistresses will leave you; so remember this: the moment one's left in the lurch there's nothing so easy as to be branded with ridicule. After that, in the eyes of the other women of the place, a man's no good for anything but to be thrown to the dogs. Within twenty-four hours after you've been dropped flat, make a declaration to another woman; for want of anyone better, make it to a chambermaid." . . . How happy I should have been, had I remembered the counsels of that great tactician! What successes lost! What humiliations received!

STENDHAL, *Memoirs of an Egotist*

Star sapphires, which reflect six rays of light from the top of the stone, were prized in antiquity as love amulets, for six is the number of Venus. . . . Pennsylvania German girls believe that they will marry the man of whom they are thinking as they swallow a four-leafed clover or a raw chicken heart. . . . Prunes [once considered an aphrodisiac] were served free of charge in Elizabethan brothels as a convenience to customers.

EDWARD S. GIFFORD, JR., *The Charms of Love*

Every club has a voluminous list of rules, dealing with, it would seem, every possible contingency . . . but nothing is entirely watertight, as the Carlton discovered. . . . A member of the club had booked a room, taken a lady of the town to bed with him and ordered a couple of whiskies. The porter promptly contacted the secretary, who hurried along in the greatest indignation. The member was completely unabashed. "What rules are there which say that you cannot take a lady into your bedroom? You know very well there is none." Turning to the porter who had followed the secretary, he added, "Now hurry up with the whiskies at once."

CHARLES GRAVES, *Leather Armchairs*

When the girl's family showed him the door with the words "Your persistence is disgusting," Vincent Van Gogh turned to the lamp on the table, put his hand into the flame, and said, "Let me see her, then, for just as long as I can hold my hand in this flame."

ARISTOTLE DELANCEY, *Van Gogh*

The only woman worth seeing undressed is one you have undressed yourself.

THE DUCHESS OF WINDSOR

You can always handle another woman if your husband is after her, but you can't handle another man.

IB.

The average male thinks about sex every 11 minutes while he's awake.

DR. PATRICK GREENE, in *Forum*

Shakespeare

In Jules Janin's translation of Macbeth, "Out, out, brief candle," becomes "Sortez, chandelle!"—"Leave, candle!" Someone else renders "so woe-begone" (Northumberland's phrase in Henry IV) as "*ainsi, douleur! Va-t'en!*"—"so, grief, be off with you!"

Facts and Fancies for the Curious

Dr. Samuel Johnson's dictionary illustrates the use of the word "confection" with this passage:

> Of best things then what world shall yield confection
> To liken her?
>
> SHAKESPEARE

There is no such passage in Shakespeare.

To understand Shakespeare well, an Englishman must come to Germany.

AUGUST SCHLEGEL

Shakespeare and golf:

Four rogues in buckram let drive at me.

1 Henry IV

Thou bleeding piece of earth.

Julius Caesar

Give me the iron.

King John

And drinking:

> Come, come, and sit you down: you shall not budge;
> You go not, till I set you up a glass.
>
> *Hamlet*

> I have yet room for six scotches more.
>
> *Antony and Cleopatra*

James T. Field, an American who came to Shakespeare late in life, declared, "There are not twenty men in Boston who could have written those plays."

Punch, April 1964

According to Spevack's *Concordance*, there are 29,066 different words in Shakespeare's works.

SHAKESPEARE QUIZ

(ANSWERS ON NEXT PAGE)

1. Did he mention America?
2. God?
3. Jesus Christ?
4. Who was the merchant of Venice?
5. Was Romeo a Capulet or a Montague?
6. Was Cymbeline a man or a woman?
7. What is the name of Juliet's nurse?
8. Which character was born at sea?
9. How many different Antonios are there in the plays?

SHAKESPEARE QUIZ *(Answers)*

1. Once: *The Comedy of Errors*: “Where America, the Indies?”
2. Many, many times.
3. Perhaps a dozen times.
4. Antonio.
5. A Montague.
6. A king of Britain.
7. Angeline.
8. Marina, in *The Tempest*.
9. Five.

Similes from the Boondocks

Grinning like a mule eating briers.

Albany, Ga.

A steak as big as a blacksmith's apron.

Like a dog hates a door.

Happy as a bee martin with a fresh bug.

She lied as easy as peas rolling off a cowhide.

Sad as a whore's baby.

Crazy as a bessie-bug. (I have no idea what a bessie-bug is).

Easy as slapping a sick baby off a chamber pot.

Red as a swamp coon's ass in dewberry time.

Thomasville, Ga.

Impatient as a poor boy at a picnic, waiting for a barefoot dance.
Hot as two hells in a quart jug.
Like trying to mix thunder and black gum.

H. GATES LLOYD

His hand was as cold as a well rope.

As gant as a ladder. (Gant = gaunt.)

She took off like a turpentined mare over a five-bar gate.

He jumped for the rum jug like a bullfrog for a red rag.

As sharp as the little end of nothing.

As tough as a strap.

FRUITY METCALFE, of Col. the Hon. Freddy Cripps

Off like Kelly's coat when the Dutchman called him a bastard.

F. C. NORRIS

Shaking like a whore in church.

C. B. B.

More friends than a jailhouse cat.

Ahoskie, N.C.

As crazy as a peach orchard boar. (I've seen half a dozen explanations of this one, none of them plausible.)

Listening to her was like drowning.

Busy as a lamp bug.

JOHN STEINBECK

As friendly as a kettle.

Small Comforts and Satisfactions

Opening the dictionary or the telephone directory to the right page.

Being told, "I checked it, and you were right." (Correction: This is a *large* satisfaction.)

To do a good action by stealth, and to have it found out by accident.

CHARLES LAMB

Seeing one's name printed in a complimentary context and spelled correctly.

Having one's cigarette lighter flame on the first flick.

A good scratch, a good sneeze.

Putting on a suit you haven't worn for some time and finding a few coins in the pockets.

Being a party—or even a witness—to a rousing good coincidence.

Having someone in a foreign city accost you and request directions.

Making a wild guess at the identity of a wine and hitting it.

Fleece-lined bedroom slippers on a frosty morning.

Watching the odometer turn up a row of the same five digits.

Realizing, on December 21, that the days are getting longer.

Being asked by a headwaiter, "Your usual table, sir?"

Bringing the last morsels of toast, butter, and marmalade out exactly even.

Catching the point of a joke told in a foreign language.

Getting back into bed on a cold night.

Having a red traffic light turn green as you approach it, and having a car vacate a parking space just ahead of you.

Small Men

Small man: good dancer, good thief.

Portuguese maxim

Tom Dewey looks like the groom on a wedding cake.

Attributed to ALICE LONGWORTH

Smiley quickly noticed that he had a quality rare among small men: the quality of openness.

JOHN LE CARRÉ, *A Murder of Quality*

Good things come in small packages.

Small men's boast

[Queen Elizabeth to Robert Cecil:] "Must! Is *must* a word to be addressed to Princes? Little man, little man! Thy father, if he had been alive, durst not have used that word." [Cecil was "small and pale and crooked of figure."]

J. P. GREEN, *A Short History of the English People*

A joke from my childhood: Who were the two smallest men in the Bible? Answer: Bildad the Shuhite (Job 2:11) and Peter, who slept on his watch.

When Mr. and Mrs. Frederick C. Little's second son arrived . . . he was not much bigger than a mouse. . . . He was only about two inches high. . . . [They] named him Stuart, and Mr. Little made him a tiny bed out of four clothespins and a cigarette box.

E. B. WHITE, *Stuart Little*

Just a span and half a span
From head to heel was this little man.
Scarce a capful of small bones
Raised up erect this Midget once.
Yet not a knuckle was askew;
Inches for feet God made him true;
And something handsome put between
His coal-black hair and beardless chin. . . .

WALTER DE LA MARE,
Ding Dong Bell

He's a little man, that's his trouble. Never trust a man with short legs—brains too near their bottoms.

NOËL COWARD

The most famous small man in history, and the greatest star in the annals of show business, was Charles Sherwood Stratton of Bridgeport, Ct., better known as "General Tom Thumb." With P. T. Barnum's encouragement, he married another midget, Mercy Lavinia Warren Bump, better known as "Mercy Lavinia," of Middleboro, Mass., on February 10, 1863. The General's best man was a third midget, George Washington Morrison Nutt, of Manchester, N.H., better known as "Commodore Nutt." The vital statistics of the wedding party were:

	Age	*Height*	*Weight*
Mercy Lavinia	21	32 inches	29 pounds
The General	24	35 inches	47 pounds
The Commodore	18	20 inches	24 pounds

Smells

Sweet as a musk-rose upon new-made hay.

KEATS

The smell of fish threw Erasmus into a fever.

Many cities have a powerful characteristic smell. Lisbon smells of coffee; Tromsö, of smoked fish; Rome, of stale urine; Brussels, of hot cooking oil; Raleigh, of tobacco; Hershey, Pennsylvania, of chocolate; Helsinki, of wood sap. But Cologne outsmells them all. According to Coleridge,

> In Köln, a town of monks and bones,
> And pavements fanged with murderous stones,
> And rags, and hags, and hideous wenches;
> I counted two and seventy stenches,
> All well defined, and several stinks!
> Ye Nymphs that reign o'er sewers and sinks,
> The river Rhine, it is well known,
> Doth wash your city of Cologne;
> But tell me, Nymphs!, what power divine
> Shall henceforth wash the river Rhine?

The smell of hot dogs made Ethel Barrymore deathly sick, and whenever she took her children to Coney Island, she brought along three handkerchiefs saturated with Atkinson's White Rose and breathed through them.

> Smells are surer than sounds or sights
> To make your heart-strings crack—

They start those awful voices o' nights
  That whisper, "Old man, come back!"
That must be why the big things pass
  And the little things remain,
Like the smell of the wattle by Lichtenberg,
  Riding in, in the rain.

KIPLING, "Lichtenberg"

When Gulliver came home from the land of the noble horselike Houyhnhnyms, he could not abide the smell of his fellowmen; it reminded him of the horrible manlike Yahoos.

Smiles

His devil prompted Barr-Saggott to smile. Now horses used to shy when Barr-Saggott smiled.

KIPLING, "Cupid's Arrows"

Sir Robert Peel's smile is like the silver fittings on a coffin.

DANIEL O'CONNELL

Frederick Locker-Lampson described Charles Lamb's smile as one "of peculiar sweetness."

What is the longest word in the English language? Answer: smiles, because there is a mile between its first letter and its last.

Venerable conundrum

The word *smile* does not occur in the Bible.

A sort of writhing movement behind the moustache showed that Sir Aylmer was smiling.

P. G. WODEHOUSE, *Uncle Dynamite*

Her smile seemed to make the world on the instant a sweeter and better place. Policemen, when she flashed it on them after being told the way somewhere, became of a sudden gayer, happier policemen and sang as they directed the traffic. Beggars, receiving it as a supplement to a small donation, perked up like magic and started to bite the ears of passers-by with an abandon which made all the difference. And when they saw that smile even babies in their perambulators stopped looking like peevish poached eggs and became almost human.

IB., *Sam the Sudden*

Giving me the sort of weak smile Roman gladiators used to give the Emperor before entering the arena, Gussie trickled off.

IB., *Right Ho, Jeeves*

There is a snake in thy smile, my dear.

SHELLEY, Song from *The Cenci*

Before [Princess Mary's] engagement to Prince Eddy [King Edward VII's elder son], she had practised for hours on end before a mirror the small Royal smile that she wore on every state or Royal occasion thereafter.

ANNE EDWARDS, *Matriarch*

Snobs

An Englishman: "Natives begin at Calais."

An American, of a Chicago multimillionaire: "He has about a hundred and fifty million dollars in bank stocks, but of course, the *bulk* of his fortune is in real estate."

A New York lady: "I hate the ocean! I always get seasick—except in yachts."

An elderly Long Island gentleman: "Know why you never see a grandmother on Long Island? They're all back home in Dallas or Dayton."

A Philadelphia man: "Everyone has a pet economy, a pet laxative, and a pet cure for hiccups."

In Franz Josef's day, you couldn't be invited to a court ball unless your family escutcheon showed *sechzehn Ahnen*—sixteen heraldic quarterings, signifying that all your great-grandparents were nobly born.

A native of Greenville, S.C.: "We got us a rat nass little town down heah, if'n the Baptists and the English sparrers don't tek it away f'um us."

Emerald Cunard: "Christmas is only for servants," and "Christ had a very unpleasant face, and John the Baptist's was little better."

The late Professor Max Müller, of Oxford: "The nicest emperor I know is Germany."

A lady named Stewart, on being asked if her family descended from the kings of Scotland: "No. *They* are descended from *us*."

A New York lady: "*She* has taken up Moral Rearmament? Rearming *her* morals would be like rearming the Galápagos Islands."

A lady in Paris of a lady of high fashion: "If she cut her finger, she'd have it dressed by Yves Saint Laurent."

When the first doctor was admitted to membership in Boodle's Club, London, some years ago, several members resigned in protest: "A professional man in *Boodle's*? Unthinkable!"

An English officer's summary of World War II: "My *dear*, the *noise*! And the *people*!"

The social aristocracy of Harvard consists of the men from the private schools. They are a small minority; but they dominate. A man may be a nice man, *and* he may be a good athlete; but unless he has been to a private school it will not help him in the day of social judgement. I had friends in the Harvard football team who came from public schools. The men from the private schools who played in the same team with them did not speak to them in the streets.

H. W. GARROD, *The Study of Good Letters*

A fanatical social climber, observing that all round the Palace of Versailles it stank of urine, told his own tenants and servants to come and make water round his château.

Quoted from Sébastien Chamfort, in Jasper Griffin's Introduction to his compilation *Snobs*

I can tell everything I want to know about a man by the way he sits on a horse.

THE FIFTH EARL OF LONDSDALE

The Earl of Durham said he considered £40,000 a year a moderate income—such a one as a man *might jog on with.*

Letter of Thomas Creevey, September 13, 1821

The Dowager Duchess of Beaufort, who died in 1889, used to thank Heaven that she had never driven in a hack-coach nor sat in the pit at the play.

GEORGE W. E. RUSSELL, *An Onlooker's Note-Book*

The Croys are one of the oldest families in Europe. I am told that there are two pictures in the Croy Palace at Brussels which reach the apogee of family pride. The first depicts Noah embarking on his Ark. On what is technically called a "bladder" issuing from his mouth are the words (in French, spoken to his sons), "Whatever you do, don't forget to bring with you the family papers of the Croys." The other picture represents the Madonna and Child, with the then Duke of Croy kneeling in adoration before them. Out of the Virgin Mary's mouth comes a "bladder" with the words (again in French), "But please put on your hat, dear Cousin!"

LORD FREDERIC HAMILTON,
The Vanished Pomps of Yesterday

Archdeacon Cox (1789) inquired whether anyone "in the least conversant in letters is unacquainted with the celebrated names *Oecolampadiu*, *Amerbach*, *Buxtorf*, *Westein*, *Iselin*."

I, for one.

[Regency London.] Mr. S—— was once riding in the Park with the Marquis of C——, then one of the kings of the fashionable world, and some other dandies of that day, when they met a respectable-looking elderly man, who nodded somewhat familiarly to S——. "Who's your friend?"

drawled Lord C——. "That?" replied S——; "Oh, a very good sort of a fellow, one of my Cheshire farmers." It was his own father; a most amiable and excellent man, and who had better blood in his veins than any of the lordlings by whom his unworthy son was surrounded.

The Reminiscences and Recollections of Captain Gronow

From the Foreword by the Duke of Devonshire to *The Gentlemen's Clubs of London* by Anthony Lejeune:

"Years ago my paternal grandfather provided a perfect example of inverted snobbism. During his latter years he became very eccentric and, alas, bad tempered. However, as a good Whig, he patronised Brooks's [Club, the Whig stronghold], where he used to sit in the magnificent hall with his stick, the end of which was filled with lead. He would place himself so that he could strike any members he disliked as they entered, so that most had to run the gauntlet of being struck a heavy blow across the shin or calf. Such is snobbism that those whom my grandfather saw fit not to strike became resentful and it became the 'in' thing to be struck by the Duke of Devonshire."

[Lady Diana Cooper, on learning that her chauffeur was laid up with a stomach ache:] "I do think servants should not be ill. We have quite enough illness ourselves without them adding to the symptoms."

PHILIP ZIEGLER, *Diana Cooper*

A prudish lady in Richmond, reporting that her niece had given birth to triplets: "Augusta's baby came today. And two others."

Mr. James Barney told me about going to a large and elegant dinner in New York, "given by a pretentious ass." When the ladies had left the table, Mr. Barney said, the butler poured a glass of old brandy for each of the gentlemen, murmuring as he poured, "The sixty-one, sir. . . . The sixty-one, sir. . . ." The host, served last, sipped, sipped again, and cried in dismay, "This is *not* the sixty-one! It's the seventy-four!"

"Good God!" said Mr. Barney, pretending to shudder. "I nearly drank it!"

His Mamma often took him on her Knee and told him how one of his Ancestors turned the Water into Long Island Sound.

GEORGE ADE

Back at the turn of the century, a set of fashionable young men-about-Paris used to top off their evenings with a call at Marcel Proust's apartment, where they'd sit and smoke and chat and sip champagne until their host sent them home. Prominent in the group was the young Duc de Guiche, son of the Duc de Gramont, and later father of Comte Charles de Gramont, who told me this story:

Proust took De Guiche aside and said, "I hear your father is giving a big shooting party at Vallière [one of his châteaus] next week, and that a lot of royalty will be present. I want very much to describe a party like that in my new book. Could you get me invited? I'll stay out of the way. Nobody needs know I'm there."

De Guiche coaxed the invitation from his reluctant father, and all went smoothly until the big luncheon that ended the party. As was traditional, the guest book was handed along the table. Everyone signed—royalty with the sprawling, saw-toothed signatures that it affects, each lustrous name followed by a gracious word or two: "Edward—capital sport!"; "Wilhelm—wunderbar!"; "Albert—merci infiniment!"

The nearer the book drew to Proust, at the foot of the table, the more visibly nervous the Duc de Gramont became. What wildly presumptuous attempt at camaraderie might not this little man, intoxicated by the heady signatures on the same page, dare to write after his own? Presently the Duc could stand the suspense no longer. He called, "*S'il vous plaît, Monsieur Proust, seulement votre nom! Pas de sentiments!*"

I have seen the book and the stark "M. Proust."

Gladys [Duchess of] Marlborough had known Proust for years. She said that his snobbishness was just snobbishness and that there was little more to say about it. He would repeat names to himself succulently. Once she said to him that she thought the Duke of Northumberland had a lovely name. He was very excited. "*Tiens*," he exclaimed, "*je vais l'annoncer*." And he got up, flung the door open and yelled, "*Madame la Duchesse de Northumberland!*"

HAROLD NICOLSON, *Diaries and Letters*

For real, rolling, resounding magniloquence, Proust should have announced the Windsor family's cousin Princess Bathildis Amalgonda of Schaumburg-Lippe.

On the death of Queen Victoria's beloved Battenberg son-in-law, someone reminded her that they would meet again in Abraham's bosom. "I will *not* meet Abraham," replied the Queen. "*Nothing* will *induce* me to meet Abraham!"

Lady Mary——, though nobly born, was not a person [Beau Brummell] desired to marry. "What could I do but cut the connection?" he observed to an intimate. "I discovered that Lady Mary actually ate cabbage!"

PETER QUENNELL, "George Bryan Brummell"

Evelyn Waugh, declining a proposed interview by Edmund Wilson: "I don't think that Americans have much to say that is of interest, do you?"

Social Maxims

Always be polite to girls. You never know whom they may become.

Punch, August 1872

Never comment on a likeness.

Apropos this, the Duchess de La Rochefoucauld once remarked to a French aristocrat, when observing that the most prominent feature of an unknown girl bore a striking similarity to his own, "God forgives, the world forgets, but the nose remains."

ANDREW SINCLAIR, *The Last of the Best*

Lord Ribblesdale . . . told me, when I was too young to believe him, that it was gentlemanly to get one's quotations very slightly wrong. In that way one unprigged oneself and allowed the company to correct one.

DIANA COOPER, *The Light of Common Day*

I find much the best way of getting on in society is never to be able to understand why anybody is to be disapproved of.

AUGUSTUS J. C. HARE,
Attributed to "a son of Canon Blakesly"

Always go to the lavatory when you have a chance.

KING GEORGE V to
EDWARD PRINCE OF WALES

Before anything else, make certain that there is toilet paper.

Never, *never* let young children answer the telephone.

A worldling, a boudoir Diogenes, has observed that it is desirable to associate with the highest, not because the highest are the best, but because, if you become disgusted with them, you can at any time descend; but that if you begin with the lower, woe unto you, for the ascent is well-nigh impossible. In the grand theater of human life a box-ticket carries one all over the house.

FREDERICK LOCKER-LAMPSON, *My Confidences*

When the pictures hang crooked, it's a sign of a good housekeeper.

Lady Charlemont said, "Whenever I make a *very* naughty quotation from *Don Juan*, I always preface it by saying, 'As Dr. Walls so touchingly observes—'"

AUGUSTUS J. C. HARE, *The Story of My Life*

[When visiting] the country houses of England, [Augustus Hare] found he made himself welcome by keeping a rule which may be commended. He always took his leave over-night in order to slip away without fuss in the morning.

SHANE LESLIE, *Men Were Different*

I have made it a rule to quit those persons I loved, when doomed to separate, without announcing the precise hour of departure.

Memoirs of William Hickey, edited by Peter Quennell

It is traditional in England for butlers to wear neither spectacles or moustaches.

Never ask a gentleman if he is from Virginia. If he is, he will find a way of letting you know. If he is not, you will embarrass him.

Anon.

Never try to give anyone road directions in the presence of a third person.

A hole in your sock may have just occurred; not so with a darn.

LORD CHESTERFIELD, *Letters*

One day [Lady Stanley's] maid told her that there was a regular uproar downstairs about precedence, as to which of the maids was to come in first to prayers. "Oh, *that* is very easily settled," said Lady Stanley: "the ugliest woman in the house must always have the precedence."

AUGUSTUS J. C. HARE, *The Story of My Life*

Married harmony can survive if the wife chooses the mistress, but it never begins if the mistress is allowed to choose the wife.

SHANE LESLIE, *George the Fourth*

Never play cards with a man called "Doc"; never eat at a place called "Mom's"; never go to bed with a woman who has more troubles than you have.

NELSON ALGREN

If you are ever tempted to make a confidential aside in a foreign language, never assume that no one else within earshot can understand it.

Love may be blind, but the neighbors aren't.

THOMAS MALLON, *A Book of One's Own*

One may talk about one's tooth, but never about one's teeth, or about one's foot, but never about one's feet. Groucho Marx's solution was to say, "My left foot hurts. So does my right foot."

Sport

In the first modern Olympic Games (1896), the big race was run from the Greek village of Marathon to the stadium in Athens—about twenty-five miles. In the 1900 Games (Paris) and again in 1904 (St. Louis), the courses also were about that length. The 1908 race (London) was the one that changed those *abouts* to an exact distance. The start was to be from Windsor Castle, and Queen Alexandra was to give the signal. The day being exceptionally hot, the starting line was drawn in a shady area, so that the Queen and the royal grandchildren would be comfortable. From there to the finish line in the White City stadium proved to be 26 miles 385 yards, and this has been the official distance ever since.

Captain Machell could vault over a billiard table without touching the lights above it, and could jump onto a mantelpiece and stand there.

THE DUKE OF PORTLAND,
Memories of Racing and Hunting

A dove-shoot is more shoot than doves.

DR. TAYLOR ROWE

[Tibor Rakassyi's account of shooting parties on the estate of a certain bachelor uncle of his on the borders of Hungary and Bohemia:] They shot partridges and hares all day, there would be a wonderful lunch spread upon tables in the shade of the acacia trees and a peasant band to play to them while they ate it, and then in the evenings, after dinner, every bachelor when he went up to bed would find a peasant girl from the village, ordered in for the night by the superintendent, tucked up there waiting for him.

ISABEL COLEGATE, *The Shooting Party*

Count Westphal . . . was not only the greatest gentleman jockey, but a hero. At a famous race, where he was to ride the horse of Count Furstenberg, he fell, breaking his collarbone and his left arm; he picked himself up and managed to remount his horse. He held the reins in his mouth, and with the unbroken arm walloped the horse, got in first, and then fainted away. It was the pluckiest thing ever seen, and won for him not only the race, but the greatest fame and his Countess, who made him promise never to ride in a race again, and he never has.

LILLIE DE HEGERMANN-LINDENCRONE,
The Courts of Memory

Before the beautiful Empress Elisabeth of Austria-Hungary went riding, she would be sewn into her habit, to ensure a smooth, perfect fit.

Guide, in a goose blind at the Curles' Neck marsh, Virginia: "Here come one lone solitary single, flyin' all by hissef!"

Old Mr. McGrath told me that when he was stunt-shooting for Winchester, he never cleaned the barrels of his shotgun from one year to the next. "A foul barrel throws a better pattern," he said.

News letter dated May 15 [1690], They saith this week was caught in the Thames a salmon 8 feet and nine inches long, which was presented by the Lord Mayor to his majesty.

ANTHONY À WOOD

Richard Toomer, who owned Slut the gun pig (see Nature Notes, page 157) was a famous marksman. Using a solid ball, not pellets, he once killed six pigeons with ten shots. A favorite feat of his was to take aim at "a small object," then invite someone to blindfold him; when he fired, he almost always hit his target.

Lord Walsingham and Lord Ripon were the two greatest shots in England. Walsingham once killed 1,070 grouse in one day (August 30, 1888). Ripon, in fifty-six years of shooting (1867–1923), killed 124,193 partridges and 241,924 pheasants, as well as thousands and thousands of other game birds. He shot so quickly and accurately that he once killed twenty-eight pheasants in a minute, and once he had seven dead birds in the air at the same time.

JONATHAN GARNIER RUFFER
Condensed from *The Big Shots*

The great Tom Sayers, the [heavyweight boxing] Champion of England, was a bricklayer's labourer and the constant throwing of bricks had given him tremendous muscles and a right-hand punch called "the auctioneer" (going... going... *gone*).

SIR RICHARD JACKSON, *Occupied with Crime*

In 1800 a Colonel Thornton bet that he could bag 400 head of game (snipe, partridges, pheasants, hares, woodcock) with 400 shots. He bagged 417 head with 411.

In the evenings after dinner, [Peter] Jackson [a bare-knuckled fighter] would amuse [Lord Lonsdale's] guests by throwing right-hand punches at the tall candles on the dining-room table. So accurate was he that he could extinguish the flames without touching the candle.

DOUGLAS SUTHERLAND, *The Yellow Earl*

The Scottish term *to do a McNab* means "to kill a salmon, a brace of grouse and a stag all in the same day."

In 1886 the famous English gunsmith James Purdey built a twenty-bore shotgun that had four barrels, arranged like two pairs of over-and-under barrels side by side. The ordinary twenty-bore weighs about 5 pounds 11 ounces; this one weighs 7 pounds 15½ ounces. It is still on view at Purdey's shop in South Audley Street, London.

In 1981 a Canadian high jumper named Arnie Boldt cleared 6 feet 8¼ inches, despite having only one leg.

Fly-fishing is to bait-fishing as seduction is to rape.

ROBERT TRAVER

Superstitions

Superstition: from *superstare,* "to stand over or near a thing, in amazement, dread, religious awe, or scruple."

People born on Christmas Day or Good Friday have the power to command spirits.

> To change the name and not the letter.
> Is a change for the worse, and not for the better.

Wallis Warfield divorced Win Spencer and married Ernest Simpson, then divorced him and married the Duke of *W*indsor. But a superstition she did observe was the one that holds peacock feathers unlucky. In *The Windsor Story* the Duchess has told how a friend innocently sent her a peacock-feather fan, when she was married to Spencer, a naval aviator: "I ran out and put it on the gate, for someone to find and take away. I was *convinced* that if I kept it, Win would be killed that very day."

In hotels Dickens wheeled his bed so that he would lie north and south.

King Edward VII would not allow his mattress to be turned on a Friday.

When Nicola Tesla, the electrical genius, stayed at a hotel, he insisted that his room number be divisible by 3; nor would he eat a morsel of food until he had calculated its cubic contents.

Seventy-five years ago, the house that stood on the northeast corner of Park Avenue and Thirty-eighth Street, New York City, suffered a series of unaccountable minor calamities—chimneys caught fire, woodwork split, wallpaper peeled; mirrors and pictures fell—until the owner concluded that his lares were losing a battle against the poltergeist inherent in his address, 67 Park, since the digits total an ominous 13. Accordingly, he requested—and was given—an address on the side-street, 101 East 38th. The poltergeist added the new digits, chuckled, and continued his mischief until the house was torn down and replaced by the apartment building that stands there now.

Chopin dreaded the number 7 so much that he refused to live in a house bearing that number, nor would he compose music or start a trip on the seventh of the month.

Queen Victoria was as cravenly superstitious as any Neapolitan midwife. Coincidences impressed her; dreams frightened her; her diaries and letters are studded with *Unberufen!* ("Touch wood!"), and at the great milestones of life—birth, marriage, death—she simply shed her title "Defender of the Faith," and became something between an astrologer and a witch doctor.

When the death of her daughter "Vicky's" uncle-in-law, King Frederick William IV of Prussia, seemed to be approaching *pari passu* with the birth of her second child, Queen Victoria wrote her: "Upon no account supposing the poor King were to die before a certain event must you see him after death. It might do a great deal of harm."

After the child was born, Victoria wrote her again, warning her that it was important for her to walk four steps *down*stairs before ever walking *up*.

She never allowed one of her children to marry in May; it was too unlucky. Leopold I of Belgium and Princess Charlotte had married in May, so had Pedro of Portugal and Stephanie, so, preeminently, had her father and mother; and death had quickly claimed one of each couple. The fourteenth of a month—any month— was also perilous. At first it was only the fourteenth of December, the date of her husband's death, in 1861, but when her daughter Princess Alice of Hesse-Darmstadt died on December 14 (1878), the

Queen's dread intensified. "This terrible day come round again!" she wrote in her *Journal*. Then her grandson Prince Albert Victor ("Prince Eddy") died on January 14 (1892), so *all* fourteenths became dire.

To round out her calendar of dreaded month and dreaded day of the month, she also had a dreaded day of the week: Saturday. George II, George III, and George IV all had died on a Saturday; so had her mother, her husband and Princess Alice; inevitably she, too, would die on that day. Actually she died on a Tuesday.

Winston [Churchill] criticized Kitchener's action in allowing the sacred shrine of the Mahdi [the late Mohammedan leader who had captured Khartoum in 1885] to be destroyed after the battle of Omdurman, 1898. . . . In the East the desecration of religious leaders' graves was supposed to attract the vengeance of the dead, under the formal curse that the desecrator would perish through the water floods, and the place of his sepulchre would not be known. This certainly occurred in the case of Kitchener [who was lost at sea when the cruiser *Hampshire* struck a mine and sank, in June 1916].

SHANE LESLIE, *Long Shadows*

"Con men are superstitious the same as anyone else," said one grifter. "I was always told that if my left hand itched, I should rub it on the seat of my pants and I'd win at faro bank. I tried it out hundreds of times and something always went wrong. Then, meeting a cross-eyed mark [sucker] is bad luck. Professional thieves don't work on rainy days. I always avoid a harelipped bates [victim]. Redheaded girls are poison to some thieves. Giving money to a plinger [beggar] is always good luck. I always spit over my left shoulder when I see a dick so he won't shake me down. If your train is late, you'll get a touch sure. There are many more, but I don't recall them, as I was never superstitious."

DAVID W. MAURER, *The American Confidence Man*

[Some Irish have] a superstition that the last person buried in a churchyard has to carry water to allay the thirst [in purgatory] of all those previously buried there. So, if there are to be two funerals at the same place on the same day, the lively competition as to which shall get first into the churchyard not unfrequently leads to a fight. Peasants have been known to put shoes or boots into coffins to save the feet of their relatives in their long and weary water-carrying walks.

W. R. LE FANU. *Seventy Years of Irish Life*

The robin is, as is well known, a blessed bird in Ireland, and no one would kill or hurt one, partly from love, partly from fear. The Irish believe that if they killed a robin a large lump would grow on the palm of their right hand. It is fear alone, however, that saves a swallow from injury, for it is equally well known that every swallow has in him three drops of the devil's blood.

IB.

Napoleon believed that his destiny was entwined with the letter *M*. For instance, six of his marshals were Masséna, Mortier, Marmont, Macdonald, Murat, and Moncey. Among his most brilliant battles were Montenotte, Mantua, Millesimo, Mondovi, Marengo, Malta, Mont Thabor, Montmirail, Montereau, Méry. And so on.

Mistletoe must be cut with a gold knife six days after the new moon.

EDWARD S. GIFFORD, JR., *The Charms of Love*

Some southerners believe that if you snip off the last inch of a puppy's tail and bury it under your doorstep, the dog may stray or be stolen, but he'll always return home.

Of the three most superstitious groups in the world—gamblers, Gypsies, and peasants—the first are said to be the worst.

In superstitious Vienna your good luck for the New Year is guaranteed if on *Sylvester* (New Year's Eve), you are dining in a restaurant on a dish of pork with dark bread and horseradish sauce, and a chimney sweep brings in a live shoat and invites you to touch it. Chimney sweeps, pigs, mushrooms, and fish are powerful jujus to the Viennese. *Bleifiguren* are another; these are small leaden figures, about an inch high, representing lanterns, dogs, chamber pots, apples, hearts, bells, and so on. Every pushcart in town has them on sale before the New Year. Buy one, put it in a spoon, and hold the spoon over a candle. When the lead melts, dump it into cold water, and the shape it congeals to symbolizes your fortune for the coming year.

The French believe it is bad luck to plant parsley on a Good Friday.

Napoleon's first wife, Josephine, believed that drinking Chambertin would help her conceive a son. It didn't.

Creole superstitions: When you move a cat to another house, put an ear of corn into the sack with it, to break the spell. . . . Don't sing before breakfast, nor on Friday or Saturday until past noon, nor in bed, nor while going to bed. . . . Bring a broom into the house only through a window. . . . The best days for painting a house are the 6th, 7th, 8th, 16th and 17th. . . . A dream of pulling a tooth means death is coming.

Gumbo Ya-Ya

The Hôtel de Paris in Monte Carlo has no bedroom number 13, 113, or 213.

If you trim your nails on a Sunday, you will become ill before the next Sunday, and if you trim them at night, you will not be at your parents' deathbeds.

It is bad luck to drop a book and not step on it, or to bring eggs into the house after sunset, or to bring in logs of locust wood at any time.

The Duque de Alva has all sorts of queer tricks and mannerisms which he practices when he thinks himself unobserved, and at which the Empress [Eugénie] laughs unmercifully, hoping thereby to shame him out of them. I noticed one day that he dropped his napkin at table and stooped to pick it up, several times. After dinner, the Empress explained that he feels he must touch his knee to the floor at least once during the meal. If he is prevented, he seems miserably preoccupied and will not eat, so he makes a regular practice of dropping his napkin, and in picking it up, slips his knee to the floor and is thus contented. He also tries to [step on] the lintel of any door he passes through. . . . I noticed how cleverly, when going in to dinner, he made a slight pause in the doorway until he could accomplish his end. The Empress, whose arm he had, hurried him along, and said laughingly, "Now, Carlos, I know what you are doing. Come along!"

AGNES CAREY, *Empress Eugénie in Exile*

It is bad luck to pass someone on the stairs.

ANDY CAPP

Helen Wills frequently appeared on the tennis court in two left shoes. Gene Tunney would never enter the ring first. Jack Sharkey would never let his managers pull on his righthand glove. Kid Chocolate always insisted that his left shoelace be tied at the back of his ankle. Bobby Jones wore the same pair of "lucky" knickers until they were hardly more than threads and patches.

If a rabbit crosses the road in front of you, you must take off your hat, spit in it, and put it back on.

A bridge players' superstition: The king of clubs is always singleton.

Toasts

We thank Thee for these mercies, Lord,
Sae far beyound our merits;
An' noo let Meg clear off the plates
An' Jock fetch in the speerits.

ROBERT BURNS

Here's to the bride! Here's to the groom!
Boom-diddy-boom-boom! Boom-boom, boom!

Offered by a friend of mine
at a wedding breakfast

I've drunk your health in company,
I've drunk your health alone;
I've drunk your health so many times,
I've damn near ruined my own.

ADMIRAL WILLIAM F. HALSEY'S
favorite toast

A toast in return:

A broadside for our Admiral!
Load every crystal gun!

OLIVER WENDELL HOLMES

Love bless him, joy crown him, God speed his career!

IB.

The love of our country!
The wine of other countries!
The women of all countries!

THOMAS MOORE

Min skål, Din skål,
Alla vackra flickers skål!

Swedish toast

("My health, your health,
All the pretty girls' healths!")

A: "I looks toward you!"
B: "I has your eye."
A: "I lifts my glass!"
B: "I likewise bows."

An Irish toast: "May you live all the days of your life!"

Clive of India: "Alas and alackaday [i.e., a girl and a *lakh*—100,000—of rupees a day]!"

For a party: "May the roof above us never fall in, and may we friends gathered below never fall out!"

For friendship, No. 1: "May you have the hindsight to know where you've been, and the foresight to know where you're going, and the insight to know when you've gone too far."

For friendship, No. 2: "Here's a health to your enemies' enemies!"

For a birthday: "May you live as long as you want, and never want as long as you live!"

Tributes

When the great Swedish ballerina Marie Taglioni (1804–84) made her debut with the Bolshoi in St. Petersburg in 1837, her performance so ravished the audience that a group of men among them begged for one of her slippers and cooked it and ate it (despite the risk, one would have thought, of toemaine poisoning and—credit Clifton Fadiman—a ballet-ache).

All men of worship said it was merry to be under such a chieftain [King Arthur], that would put his person in adventure as other poor knights did.

SIR THOMAS MALORY, *Morte d'Arthur*

[Sir Lancelot, of Queen Guinevere:] "Lady, I take witness of God, in you have I had mine earthly joy."

IB.

Some of the fiercest and most inflexible men the world has ever seen were in the Army of Northern Virginia. Stonewall Jackson, Jubal A. Early, John B. Gordon, J. E. B. Stuart and J. B. Hood would stand erect in any presence on earth, yet they uncovered in Lee's presence and took the law from him as a child takes it from his father. Jackson said that Lee was the only man whom he would follow blindly, but he would follow Lee wherever he chose to lead. The whole army had exactly that feeling toward "Marse Robert."

CAPT. WILLIAM L. ROYALL, C.S.A.

I have known all the great men of my time in the land . . . and many beyond it. [Edward VII] was the most kingly of them all.

LORD ESHER

After the Battle of Crécy (1346), the victorious Black Prince of England said of his dead and defeated enemy, John the Blind of Luxembourg, "The battle was not worth the death of this man."

Cassius, of Julius Caesar:

> He doth bestride the narrow world
> Like a Colossus, and we petty men
> Walk under his huge legs and peep about
> To find ourselves dishonourable graves

SHAKESPEARE, *Julius Caesar*

When they saw Helen coming along the wall, they whispered softly among themselves: "Small wonder that Trojans and well-greaved Achaeans should suffer greatly and long for such a woman, for she is marvellously like to the immortal goddesses to look upon."

HOMER, *The Iliad*

Maurice Baring, who made this translation, added, "This is the best description of female beauty in literature."

His was the straightest court there ever was and the cleanest, and King George V was the straightest man I ever knew.

SIR DEREK KEPPEL

Doubtless God could have made a better berry [than the strawberry], but doubtless God never did.

DR. WILLIAM BUTLER (1535–1618)

Dr. Watson, of Sherlock Holmes: "The best and wisest man whom I have ever known."

Sherlock Holmes, of Irene Adler: "*The* woman!"

My aunt saw a newspaper item about a Sherman tank and burst out, "I don't care if he *was*! He was a great general, and it's unpatriotic to bring it up now."

C. D. S.

Typos and Blemishes

This chapter should perhaps be headed "Parental guidance recommended." It is about misprints—"typos"; and as everyone knows, the funniest are indelicate, if not downright ribald. Anyone whom this collection offends may be comforted to learn that for every bawdy typo appearing here, I rejected a dozen far bawdier. Some of the specimens I myself spotted; others were quoted to me; but the majority I owe to my former colleagues in journalism, nearly every one of whom carries a wallet stuffed with his own collection.

In the days when type was set from copy written in pencil, many of the errors that reached print could be blamed on muddy script. For instance, the house that was credited with an astonishing "219,209 staircases" had in fact "zigzag staircases"; and a certain concert program actually included Millard's "Ave Maria," not Mulligan's "Avenue Maria," as reported. (This may have been the concert where a soprano rendered "Ballade by A Fat Major," according to the review in the next day's paper.)

Modern newspapers, with their copy no longer handwritten, blame most of their typos on mischievous compositors or on the gremlins that infest every composing room, no matter how automated. Here is a typo that may have contributed to the demise of the *Philadelphia Bulletin*: "Beethoven had ten children and practised on a spinster in the attic," but the *Washington Post* managed to survive this one: "Mrs. N—— W—— looked particularly neat and smart in her A.W.V.S. uniform after a long lay at headquarters."

The gremlins respect *no* author, however eminent. Pope Sixtus V's edition of the Vulgate swarmed with so many errors that heretics acclaimed it as disproof positive of papal infallibility. The *Oxford Book of American Literary Anecdotes* has one about Edwin Arlington Robinson's sonnet on a butcher named Reuben Bright. When Bright's beloved wife died,

> He packed a lot of things that she had made
> Most mournfully away in an old chest
> Of hers, put some chopped-up cedar boughs
> In with them, and tore down the slaughter house.

But when the sonnet was published, an "inspired printer," as Robinson called him, said that Bright "tore down *to* the slaughter house."

Charles Kegan Paul's *Memories* tells of a writer who described an area between a volcano and the sea as "strewn with erratic blocks." The printer had other ideas, and Paul was dismayed to read that it was "strewn with erotic blacks."

A poem of Alfred Noyes's described a family dreaming of their soldier coming home from the wars, while

> All night he lies beneath the stars
> And dreams no more out there,

which the *Irish Times* printed as "All night he lies beneath the stairs." On the other hand, it is quite possible that we owe to a typo one of the most evocative lines in all English poetry. Thomas Nashe's "In Time of Pestilence" has a line, "Brightness falls from the air," that may have been written "from the *hair*," thus gaining in logic what it loses in magic.

Ambiguity is responsible for some superb specimens:

The font so generously presented by Mrs. Smith will be set in position at the east end of the church. Babies may now be baptised at both ends.

Miss R——'s
Bust Unveiled
At Nearby School

Women who drive by and drop off their clothing at Blank Speed Wash will receive prompt attention.

Anchorage Daily Times

WEDDING HELD
MENACE TO SLEEP

The humor of another large group depends on accidental omissions. "The Wicked Bible" is so called because it omitted the crucial word "not" from the seventh (adultery) commandment. A news story about the capture of the USS *Pueblo* ended like this:

A new signal rose to her yardarm:
Copyright 1970 by Lloyd M. Bucher

One of my favorite typos falls into none of these categories. I can't classify it or explain it at all. I can only quote it: "Carolyn B——, who spoke on 'Looking Ahead,' said that the three qualities necessary for success are faith, determination and Charles McFee."

Lastly, two pearls from the late *New York Herald Tribune*, one scatological, the other hysterical. A headline on a sports page had been intended to read:

FOUR SHIFTS
IN YALE CREW

Unfortunately a crucial letter dropped out, and presently all Princeton and all Harvard were inquiring of all Yale if this were news.

The other treasure was given me by the *Trib*'s late city editor Stanley Walker. It involved, he said, a confusion between two stories in the same edition and their accompanying illustrations, or "cuts." One story announced the city aquarium's acquisition of a rare tropical fish; the other announced a new honor that had befallen Congressman Hamilton Fish. The make-up editor was either drowsy or inspired; he put the cut of the tropical fish over the Hamilton Fish story, and vice versa.

By the time Stanley saw what had happened, the edition was already on the streets. A moment later his phone rang. "This is Mr. Fish," a furious voice shouted. "I've never been so insulted in all my life! You can't get away with this! I'm going to sue your paper within an inch of—"

Stanley broke in, "We're terribly sorry, sir! The man responsible for that blunder has already been fired, and we're printing a full apology in our next edition. If there's anything else you'd like us to do, Congressman, you have only—"

"'Congressman'! Who the devil do you think you're talking to?"

"Why, Congressman Fish!"

"You idiot, this is Mr. Tropical Fish, and you'll be hearing from my attorneys! Good day!"

To Stanley's lasting regret, the joker never came forward and identified himself.

Forty years ago, *The Candle*, a literary monthly published at Ohio State University, ruined the point of a mild little essay of mine by garbling a salient quotation so that it came out, "The gates of hell shall now prevail."

JAMES THURBER,
"Such a Phrase as Drifts Through Dreams"

Lawrence Durrell's hilarious *Esprit de Corps* has a chapter called "Frying the Flag"—an account of an English-language newspaper, the *Central Balkan Herald,* published in Serbia by two elderly English sisters, with the "help" of non-English-speaking printers. The result was a series of absurd typos loosely held together by snatches of normal English. I'd like to quote the whole chapter, but I'll reluctantly confine myself to a few samples:

Headline: "QUEEN OF HOLLAND GIVES PANTY FOR EX-SERVICE MEN."

Sporting news: "In a last desperate spurt, the Cambridge crew, urged on by their pox, overtook Oxford."

Headline on a story about Serbia's timber resources: "BRITAIN TO BUY SERBIAN TIT-PROPS."

A local news story began: "More dogs have babies this summer in Belgrade."

And finally, the title of a gardening article: "How to Plant Wild Bubs."

Reader, *Carthagenia* was of the mind, that unto those *Three Things* which the Ancients held Impossible, there should be added this *Fourth*, to find a Book printed without *Errata's*. It seems, the Hands of *Briareus*, and the Eyes of *Argus*, will not prevent them.

COTTON MATHER, *Magnalia*

Ugliness

By all accounts [John Wilkes] was cursed from birth by a most unnatural ugliness. [Sir Joshua] Reynolds describes "his fore-head low and short, his nose shorter and lower, his upper lip long and projecting, his eyes sunken and horribly squinting." . . . However, we will accept the ugliness as Wilkes himself accepted it, bearing in mind his claim that it took him only half an hour to talk away his face, given which start he would back himself for a lady's favours against the handsomest man in England.

OLGA VENN, "John Wilkes"

A belle laide is a woman who is attractively ugly: Wilkes was a *beau laid*.

She had a face like an unplayable lie.

Anon.

Uncle John Locker was very ugly. One day at Malta he asked a stranger, who had just landed, to take wine, expressing his pleasure at seeing him there and his obligation in these words: "Yesterday, sir, I was the ugliest man in all Malta!"

FREDERICK LOCKER-LAMPSON, *My Confidences*

Sir —— is so grotesquely featured that he looks as if he were walking about doing it for fun.

IB.

The helen has been suggested as a unit of feminine pulchritude: that quantity sufficient to launch a thousand ships. The practical unit would be the quantity sufficient to launch one ship: the milli-helen. The unit of ugliness then is the antimillihelen: the quantity required to sink one battleship.

Letter to *National Review* from
CHARLES C. LITTELL, JR.

Jenny Lind's own description of her young self was "small, ugly, broad-nosed, shy, gauche, under-grown." Her favorite of all the stories by her friend Hans Christian Andersen was "The Ugly Duckling."

When two homely people meet they allus seem glad t' see each other.

KIN HUBBARD, *Abe Martin*

There are abundant stories about Lincoln's ugliness. The following (condensed from Col. Alexander K. McClure's *Abe Lincoln's Yarns and Stories*) is typical:

A man of forbidding countenance drew a revolver and thrust it into Lincoln's face.

"What seems to be the matter?" inquired Lincoln.

"Well," replied the stranger, "some years ago I swore that if I ever came across an uglier man than myself, I'd shoot him."

"Shoot me!" Lincoln said. "If I am uglier than you, I don't want to live."

He was as big as a skinned mule and twice as ugly.

Texas saying

[The actor] Charles Butterworth's ugliness was a neighborhood sensation.

ALVA JOHNSTON, in *The New Yorker*

I was in a beauty contest once. I not only came in last, I was hit in the mouth by Miss Congeniality.

PHYLLIS DILLER

The baby was so ugly, they had to hang a pork chop around its neck to get the dog to play with it.

Anon.

The first British High Commissioner of Corfu, Sir Thomas Maitland (1759?–1824), had such autocratic ways that he was widely known as "King Tom"; but more widely as "the Abortion," because of his extreme ugliness.

Vanity

Her clothes were full of Pin-holes where she had been hanging medals on herself, and she used to go into a Handball Court every Day and throw up Bouquets, letting them bounce back and hit her.

GEORGE ADE

He hated to turn out the light at Night and have all his Good Looks go to waste for Hours at a Stretch. It was like breaking Home Ties for him to say goodbye to a Mirror.

IB.

Margot Asquith's affair with herself should be stopped by the police.

DOROTHY PARKER

Frank Fay, a theatrical producer in the 1920s, was notoriously conceited. Fred Allen said of him, "The last time I saw Fay, he was walking down Lovers' Lane holding his own hand."

Lord Houghton's vanity is amusingly natural. Something was said of one of Theodore Hook's criticisms. "You know even *I* never said anything as good as that," said Lord Houghton, and quite seriously.

AUGUSTUS J. C. HARE, *The Story of My Life*

As Lady Caroline Paget, the Duchess of Cleveland used to be very proud of her little foot. She wore an anklet, and would often sit upon a table and let it fall down upon her

foot to show it.... One day Lady Isabella St. John, who was equally proud of her little foot, said, "Let me try if I can get your anklet over my foot, Lady Caroline." And she put it on, and, to Lady Caroline's great disgust, *kicked it off*, to show how easily her foot would go through it.

IB.

Lady Audrey Buller said she remembered seeing Lady Dudley Stuart, daughter of Lucien Bonaparte, as a very old lady. She was renowned for her beautiful feet and ankles, of which apparently she was inordinately proud, for it was said that she would drive through the streets of Rome with her feet hanging out of the carriage window.

LADY NORAH BENTINCK,
My Wanderings and Memories

Henry Clapp [I can't identify him] said of Horace Greeley: "He was a self-made man and worshipped his creator." Of

Dr. O——, a vain and popular clergyman, that "he was continually looking for a vacancy in the Trinity."

MRS. JAMES T. FIELDS, *Memories of a Hostess*

The Duke of Wellington's account of his one meeting with Lord Nelson: "He could not know who I was, but he entered at once into conversation with me, if I can call it conversation, for it was all on his side, and all about himself, and in, really, a style so vain and so silly as to surprise and almost disgust me. . . . He went out of the room for a moment, and I have no doubt to ask the office-keeper who I was, for when he came back, he was altogether a different man, both in manner and matter."

"I [Sherlock Holmes] followed you—"
"I saw no one."
"That is what you may expect to see when I follow you."

SIR ARTHUR CONAN DOYLE,
"The Adventure of the Bruce-Partington Plans"

Modesty is a virtue not often found among poets, for almost every one of them thinks himself the greatest in the world.

MIGUEL DE CERVANTES

When Andrew Mellon first appeared in *Who's Who*, he gave his birthdate as 1852; in the next edition, as 1854; and eventually as 1855.

[Victorien Sardou, the playwright,] was a little overgenerous in the use of I.

Paris and the Arts, 1851–1896, from the *Goncourt Journal*

YUM-YUM: Yes, I am indeed beautiful! Sometimes I sit and wonder . . . why it is that I am so much more attractive than anybody else in the whole world. Can this be vanity? No! Nature is lovely and rejoices in her loveliness. I am a child of nature and take after my mother.

W. S. GILBERT, *The Mikado*

Charles C. F. Greville, a courtier and diarist in the first part of the nineteenth century, was famous for his vanity. Disraeli said of him, "I have never witnessed the disease in so violent a form, yet I have read Cicero and I have known Lord Lytton."

You can pick out actors by the glazed look that comes into their eyes when the conversation wanders away from themselves.

MICHAEL WILDING

Verses

The chic and rich, the chic and rich,
I haven't got much to hand 'em.
They make me feel like a son of a bitch,
And I have to be drunk to stand 'em.

PHILIP BARRY

Clerihew

Said Lady Mary Wortley Montagu,
When rebuked for omitting an *accent aigu*,
"I leave diacritics
to Continentals and Semitics."

J. B., III

Inscription for the door of a W. C.:

Ici viennent tomber en ruines
Les chef d'oeuvres de la cuisine.

BRILLAT-SAVARIN

It nearly broke the family's heart
When Lady Jane became a tart,
But pride is pride, and race is race,
And so, to save the family's face,
They bought her a most exclusive beat
On the sunny side of Jermyn Street.

Author unknown (to me)

As I sat in the café I said to myself,
They may talk as they please about what they call pelf,
They may sneer as they like about eating and drinking,
But help it I cannot, I cannot help thinking
How pleasant it is to have money, heigh-ho!
How pleasant it is to have money!

ARTHUR HUGH CLOUGH

She sif' de meal, she gimme de hus';
She bake de bread, she gimme de crus';
She fry de meat an' gimme de skin,
And dat was whah de trouble begin.

Plantation Song

O Moon, when I gaze on thy beautiful face,
Careening along through the boundaries of space,
The thought has often come into my mind
If I ever shall see thy glorious behind.

"A housemaid poet," quoted by
ROBERT ROSS in the Academy

HAMADAN

Hamadan is my native place;
And I must say in praise of it,
It merits, for its ugly face,
What everybody says of it.

Its children equal its old men
In vices and avidity;
And they reflect their babes again
In exquisite stupidity.

From an epigram of Abul fadhel
Ahmed, surnamed al-Hamadhani, recorded in D'Herbelot's
The Laughing Philosopher, 1835

Poor South! Her books get fewer and fewer.
She was never much given to literature.

J. GORDON COOGLER

I banged the door with such a slam,
It sounded like a wooden d - - n.

FREDERICK LOCKER-LAMPSON

How fortunate French lyricists are! They have *toujours* to rhyme with *amour*, and *fidèle* with *éternelle*, whereas we have little more than *dove* and *above* to rhyme with *love*. *(Shove? glove? of?* Pah!)

I never glanced at her full bust but wished myself the snake
That bit the harlot bosom of that heathen by the Nile.

Can you believe that Tennyson wrote that? He did, in something called "Happy." He also wrote this:

O plump headwaiter at the Cock,
  To which I most resort,
How goes the time? 'Tis five o'clock.
  Go fetch a pint of port.

The sonnet is perhaps the most effective soporific, in whatever language it is written.

SIR HENRY HOLLAND

Avec ses quatre dromadaires
Don Pedro d'Alfaroubeira
Courut le monde et l'admira.
Il fit ce que je voudrais faire
Si j'avais quatre dromadaires.

GUILLAUME APOLLINAIRE

He that will woo a widow must not dally,
  He must make hay while the sun doth shine,
He must not stand with her, Shall, Shall I?
  But boldly say, Widow, thou must be mine!

Anon.

The world is full of double beds
And such delightful maidenheads
  That there is simply no excuse
  For sodomy and self-abuse.

HILAIRE BELLOC

The following quatrain, source unknown, has been rattling around in my head until I've begun plucking at the coverlet. I set it down here in the shameless, selfish hope of exorcising it, even at the expense of some reader's sanity:

Dearly beloved brethren, is it not a sin
When peeling a potato, to throw away the skin?
  For the skin feeds pigs, and pigs feed you.
  Dearly beloved brethren, surely this is true?

The Very Rich

They make their money the old-fashioned way. They inherit it.

Anon.

When the manager of the hotel in Évian where the Aga Khan was residing ventured to rebuke him for an impropriety, the Aga bought the hotel and fired him.

The richest of the Indian princes, the Nizam of Hyderabad, made an intimate confidant of Sir Walter Monckton, later King Edward VIII's trusted counselor. Monckton was not easily impressed, but he never forgot being shown the blue safe where the Nizam kept his sapphires, the green safe for his emeralds, and the red for his rubies.

SIR WALTER MONCKTON, in conversation with Col. Charles J. V. Murphy

Saratoga Springs, N.Y., Aug. 7— . . . A gazebo of ribbons and tinsel enclosed the dance floor [at a party given by Mr. and Mrs. Cornelius Vanderbilt Whitney], the scene in 1887 of the noted incident in which Mr. Whitney's grandfather, William Collins Whitney, lost $385,000 at the gambling tables while waiting for his wife to dress.

New York Times, August 8, 1982

Medina al Zahra, which the first and greatest of the Spanish Caliphs, Abderraman III, began to build in 936, [was] certainly the most luxurious palace ever built in any age. Four thousand marble columns were used in its construction, and the quantity of gold, bronze and silver employed were fabulous. The Chamber of Caliphs had thirty-two doors, each decorated with gold and ivory and resting on pillars of transparent crystal. Thirteen thousand male servants lived here. The fish in the garden tanks alone consumed 12,000 loaves of bread every day.

Condensed from GERALD BRENAN, *The Face of Spain*

"Paul Getty? Why, Paul's not worth a cent more than half a billion dollars!"

CHARLES WRIGHTSMAN

Prince Tcherkasky used to have the flowers in his garden [on the French Riviera] changed every night by a noctivagant crew of 48 gardeners so that a new vista of beauty would greet his eye each morning.

LEONARD SLATER, *Aly*

Calouste Gulbenkian [the Armenian oil multimillionaire] had a Turkish chef who left and was engaged by the Turkish Ambassador in Moscow, taking with him his rolling-pin. Gulbenkian sent two detectives from Paris to fetch the rolling-pin, worth one pound at most.

NUBAR GULBENKIAN, *Pantaraxia*

Nubar Gulbenkian bought a London taxi for his personal use. "They say it can turn on a sixpence," he boasted, "whatever that is."

The late André Sella, proprietor of the Hotel du Cap d'Antibes, told me this story: "I remember one of dose rich Russians, Count Apraxine. He had many *manies* [idiosyncrasies]. One was to have sent to his salon every night a dozen fresh strawberries on a silver dish. Fresh strawberries was hard to find in Chanuary in dose days—I am talking of nineteen two, t'ree, along dere. Dey cost ten gold francs apiece, but de count, he don't care. And w'en de strawberries are browt every night, w'at you t'ink he did? He squeezèd dem wit' a fork, and w'en dey are all squeezèd, he *smell* dem. 'Ah!' he say, taking deep breat'.

'A-*ha*!' and den he go to bed. . . . No, he did not eat dem. He chust squeezèd dem. I t'ink people who have too much money, dey are alwiss a lettle crazy."

Money doesn't make you happy, but it quiets the nerves.

SEAN O'CASEY

[Prince] Agostino Chigi, who wanted to pay a compliment to Pope Leo X (1513–21), invited him to dinner and, as the courses succeeded one another, the gold plates that had just been used were thrown into the Tiber, under the eyes of the guests. Leo X was suitably impressed, but on the following day the gossip of Rome hastened to inform him that the ostentatious banker had had nets stretched under the windows, and that the complete gold set was once again in the prince's coffers. But nevertheless the effect was successful enough to be remembered five centuries later.

MAURICE RHEIMS, *The Strange Life of Objects*

Any man who knows what he's worth isn't worth much.

J. PAUL GETTY, to Cleveland Amery

About 22,000 men and women worked twenty-four hours a day for twenty-four years to build the Taj Mahal, and 100,000 men worked for twenty years to build the Pyramids.

May 15, 1879. Dined with Lord and Lady Aberdeen—a very large party, seventy-four pots of flowers upon the table.

AUGUSTUS J. C. HARE, *The Story of My Life*

. . . the plaintive cry of the Grand Duchess of Mecklenburg-Strelitz, on hearing that the Emperor of Austria was coming to stay—"What are we to do? Our poor palace has only sixty-two bedrooms."

JONATHAN GARNIER RUFFER, *The Big Shots*

Baron James de Rothschild was playing cards with the wealthy Marquis d'Aligre when the Marquis dropped a louis (a 20-franc piece, worth just under $4) on the floor and stopped the game to look for it. Rothschild said, "We mustn't lose a louis, must we?" He took a 100-franc banknote from his pocket, rolled it up and set it alight, and held it near the carpet to aid D'Aligre's search.

[Lord Frederic Hamilton was invited on a tiger hunt by the Maharajah of Cooch Behar.] Each guest had a great Indian double tent, bigger than most London drawing-rooms. The one tent was pitched inside the other, with an air-space of about one foot between to keep out the fierce sun. Every tent was carpeted with cotton, and completely furnished with dressing-tables and chests of drawers, as well as writing-table, sofa and arm-chairs. . . . The Census of 1891 was taken whilst we were in camp, so I can give the exact number of retainers whom the Maharajah brought with him. It totalled 473, including mahouts and elephant-tenders, grooms, armourers, taxidermists, tailors, shoemakers, a native doctor and a dispenser, and boatmen, not to mention the Viennese conductor and the thirty-five members of the orchestra, cooks, bakers and table waiters. The Maharajah certainly did things on a grand scale.

LORD FREDERIC HAMILTON,
Here, There and Everywhere

The Saudi Arabian Oil Minister, Ahmed Zaki al-Yamani, was having his beard trimmed at the Inter-Continental Hotel in Geneva when an urgent message called him away. He apologized to the barber and tipped him with a 500-franc note—the equivalent of $300.

PAUL LEWIS, *New York Times*

Whenever [Lord Lonsdale (1857–1944)] moved from one house to another, a special train was reserved for his household. If he travelled overnight, one first-class sleeper was reserved for himself and another for his pack of foxhounds. Along the route station masters paraded on the platforms of their stations, to see the Lonsdale train safely through, and to be rewarded with a five-pound note, handed out by Lonsdale's valet, who was required to stay up all night for the purpose.

DOUGLAS SUTHERLAND, *The Yellow Earl*

When [Lord Lonsdale's] first Mercedes arrived, he was horrified to discover that its silver work was not real silver but only chromium plate. It was put on the next boat back to Germany with instructions that all the chromium was to be replaced immediately with silver.

IB.

An Arab embarking on the Concorde's London–New York flight with three handbags was told that he might carry only one of them into the cabin; the other two would have to be checked. He preferred to buy an adjacent seat, so that the bags would not be out of his sight, as they contained, he said, $1,200,000 in U.S. currency. The cost of the seat was $1,813.

Associated Press, November 22, 1982

Despite an allowance of £50,000 a year, by the time the Prince of Wales, later King George IV, was twenty-five years old, he owed one tailor £16,774 and his perfumer £518.

[The Honorable Mrs. Heywood-Lonsdale:] "My husband went to dinner once recently where there were footmen in white gloves, the whole thing. And they were using the gold dinner plates—the hostess said she preferred to use the gold ones, because they didn't need any polishing. You just washed them up in Lux and then stacked them away, just like china."

SIMON WINCHESTER, *The Noble Lordships*

The British royal family travels in comfort. When the Duke and Duchess of Windsor went on their honeymoon in 1937, they took along 266 pieces of luggage, including 180 trunks.

And when, soon after the outbreak of World War II, it was decided to send Queen Mary to stay with her niece the Duchess of Beaufort, in the country, she brought with her 70 pieces of luggage and—to the Duchess's consternation —55 servants.

Lady Martonmere, whose husband was Governor of Bermuda from 1964 to 1972, used to tell her dinner guests at Government House that the best way to keep one's diamonds clean, she had found, was to soak them in gin.

They're so rich, their cream don't splash.

FINIS FARR

When Sir Basil Zaharoff paid his annual visit to the Hôtel de Paris in Monte Carlo, one of the most luxurious in the world, he took along his own silver, linen, china, and chef.

William Beckford (1760–1844), the author of the fantastic oriental tale *Vathek*, made frequent journeys, during which he stayed at inns, but never until his rooms had been repapered, even though his stay might be for only one night.

Thomas: "But has she got the stuff, Mr. Fag? Is she rich, hey?"

Fag: "Rich!—Why, I believe she owns half the stocks! Zounds! Thomas, she could pay the national debt as easily as I could my washerwoman! She has a lap-dog that eats out of gold,—she feeds her parrot with small pearls,—and all her thread-papers are made of bank-notes!"

RICHARD BRINSLEY SHERIDAN, *The Rivals*

Behind every great fortune there is a crime.

BALZAC

A Philadelphia lady, on taking delivery of her enormous new yacht: "But where are the elevators?"

For two and a half centuries after the reign of Peter the Great, there had been a fabulous royal town at Tsarskoe Selo, "the Czar's Village," fifteen miles south of Saint Petersburg (now Leningrad). There were two palaces. One, the Catherine Palace, was blue and white, with more than 200 rooms. It was decorated with mother-of-pearl, marble, amber, lapis lazuli, silver, and gold. The other, the less ornate Alexander Palace, had 100 rooms.

They stood on 1,680 acres of landscaped park and botanical gardens in which statues, pavilions, and kiosks were interspersed. There was a network of shaded walks, two bandstands, a parade ground, and an artificial lake for small sailboats and toy yachts. At one end of the lake was a pink Turkish bath and not far away a synthetic hill crowned by a red-and-gold Chinese pagoda. There was also a Chinese village, bridge, and theater.

GUY RICHARDS, *The Hunt for the Czar*

Seized with a mania for feeling the touch of money, [Caligula] would often pour out great piles of gold pieces in some open place, walk over them barefooted, and wallow in them for a long time with his whole body.

SUETONIUS, "Gaius Caligula"

Oddest shoot I ever saw was in Russia, in the Perm District, just beyond the Urals. Nineteen twelve. We shot all morning: snipe, white partridges, woodcock, blackcock, wolves, Siberian roebuck, and heaven knows what else. Then caviar and vodka. Then a picnic luncheon, course after course, all served on priceless Sèvres, and washed down with vintage champagne. When the tables had been cleared, the host lined up all the servants and told us. "Now we'll have some *real* shooting!" And damme if they didn't toss that Sèvres into the air for us to pot! "Shoot!" he said. "You'll enjoy it! The china's quite good quality." Imagine! Sèvres clay pigeons!

Told by the late COLONEL THE HON. FREDERICK CRIPPS

I want to wear banknotes next my skin winter and summer, ten-pound ones in the chilly months, changing to fivers as the weather gets warmer.

P. G. WODEHOUSE, *Ice in the Bedroom*

Bunker Hunt, the multimillionaire, was asked why he wanted to corner the silver market. He said, "A billion dollars ain't what it used to be."

The richer your friends, the more they will cost you.

ELIZABETH MARBURY

The architect who was designing Count Boni de Castellane's famous "Pink House" in Paris asked what sort of staircase he wanted. "Just like the one at the Opéra," Boni told him, "only larger."

When the present Duke of Westminster became engaged in 1974, someone asked him if he had anything special in mind as an engagement present for his fiancée. To this he rather shatteringly replied, "Well, I thought I might give her the North Wales coast."

HUGH VICKERS AND CAROLINE MCCULLOUGH,
Great Country House Disasters

Voices

Pierre Loti's young wife . . . has the sad voice of a sick bird, a voice which does not have the timbre of a human voice.

Paris and the Arts, 1851–1896, from the *Goncourt Journal*

[Édouard Simon Lockroy, a French politician and man of letters], has the pleasant, soft voice of a good little old man in a fairy tale.

IB.

A voice like a good brand of Burgundy made audible.

P. G. WODEHOUSE, *Cocktail Time*

Her voice was soft and tender, like that of a hen crooning over its egg.

IB., *Joy in the Morning*

She spoke in a low voice, like beer trickling out of a jug.

IB., *The Code of the Woosters*

. . . that high voice, with the intonation of a steeple-clock.

FLAUBERT

I have noticed that fat women often have soft, sweet voices.

J. V. B.

Wants

Some way to tell the driver of the car ahead that he has forgotten to switch off his turn signal.

A tiny beeper for eyeglasses, so that you can tune in and find out where you absently left them.

A desk with a slightly concave top, so that pens and pencils will roll down toward the center, instead of off onto the floor.

An effective thiefproof lock for automobiles. (Surely this shouldn't be too difficult!)

A "soberific." A drunken person takes one tablet or ounce or capsule, and is instantly sober. Apropos, I learn from Julian Street's *Table Topics* that "among the fine breads made on the Island of Rhodes was a loaf of which Lynceus of Samos declared: 'Often a man who is drunk becomes sober again by eating of it.'"

An automobile horn that seems to say, "PLEEEEEEEASE let me pass!"

Something to tell you when your watch stops.

An infallible assurance that someone is telling the truth.

Proof of the efficacy of prayer.

Weird Wagers

Th' feller that don't know what he's talkin' about allus wants t' bet you.

KIN HUBBARD, *Abe Martin*

The two most famous bettors on record are probably Jim Smiley and Phileas Fogg. According to Mark Twain, Smiley, of Calaveras County, California, lost $40 in very little more time than it took to tell two frogs "One—two—three—*git*!" And according to Jules Verne, Fogg, of Savile Row, London, won £20,000 in very little less time than precisely eighty days.

English bucks of a few generations ago would bet on anything. Like Phileas Fogg, they particularly enjoyed bets against time, especially when the element of endurance was involved. For instance:

A Captain Bennet bet that he could roll a hoop 22 miles in 3½ hours. A Mr. Lloyd bet that he could walk 30 miles backwards in 9 hours. Charles Bulpett bet that he could ride a mile, run a mile, and walk a mile within 16½ minutes. Someone else bet that he could walk 12 miles on stilts in 4½ hours, without stopping and never stepping down. Still another man bet that he could stand on one foot for 12 hours. All the principals won, though the man who had stood on one foot needed to be carried home.

The Duc de Chartres bet that he could prick 500,000 pinholes in a sheet of paper before the Comte de Genlis could go from Paris to Fountainebleau and back. I don't know the details of the bet—the date, the distance, whether Genlis was afoot or on horseback; all I know is that Genlis won easily.

These are rather simple bets, prosaic and straightforward, but there are abundant others that show imagination in either the terms of the bet or the ingenuity with which they were met. As an example of the first, I quote from the *Annual Register* for June 28, 1811: "On Tuesday, Mr. Coxetter of Newbury had two Southdown sheep shorn at his factory exactly at 5 A.M., from the wool of which a complete damson-coloured coat was made and worn by Sir John Throckmorton at 6:15 P.M., being 2¾ hours within the time allotted, for a wager of 1,000 guineas."

An unusual bet against time was made in the 1770s by the fourth Duke of Queensberry, who undertook to convey a message fifty miles within an hour—not merely the *gist* of the message but the *actual paper*. (Bear in mind that this was long before the railroad!) He won by stuffing the paper into a hollowed cricket ball, then stationing fifty expert fielders in a circle one mile in circumference, and having them toss the ball around it fifty times.

Horace Walpole described another unusual bet in a letter dated October 17, 1756: "My Lord Rockingham and my nephew, Lord Orford, have made a match for £500 between five turkeys and five geese to run from Norwich to London." Rockingham, who was driving the geese, won easily; his flock waddled along, hour after hour, whereas Orford's turkeys insisted on roosting at night.

A Yorkshireman bet that one pound of cotton could not be spun into a thread longer than two miles. Speculate on his judgment while you read about the young man who bet that he could tie a cord one mile long to a one-pound weight and draw it hand over hand, in under two and a half hours. The young man did it, but the Yorkshireman lost: The thread ran longer than twenty-three miles.

To return to bets on endurance, here is a surprising one that I found in *Handy Book of Curious Information:* "An American made a wager with an Austrian athlete that the latter could not stand a pint of water falling on his hand, drop by drop, in one spot, from a height of only three feet. The athlete's hand was lined with skin almost as thick and tough as cowhide, and all the spectators pronounced the American's bet a foolish one."

Let me interrupt. You will have guessed already that the American won, but at what point? There are 11,520 drops in a pint of water. Where did the Austrian surrender? Make your estimate, then read on: "When about 300 drops had fallen, it was apparent that [the Austrian] was suffering. At the 420th drop he gave up, declaring he could no longer endure the torture. His palm was badly swollen and rapidly inflaming, and in one spot the skin had broken, exposing raw flesh."

Another American, this time the principal, made a memorable endurance bet in 1914: G. Howell Parr of Baltimore undertook to *roll* three miles through town without stopping for longer than a minute or so. Wearing a cap, a sweater with pads on the elbows, and football pants with pads on the knees, and with his hands bandaged, he began rolling at 8 one evening and crossed the finish line at 11:10 next morning, which works out at just over seventeen feet per minute.

There is a huge field of bets like this, but with handicaps, and I have chosen two as typical. The first required endurance plus strength. In 1764 a man from Lincolnshire bet he could walk 3¼ miles in three hours, carrying a fifty-pound weight in each hand; he did it in just under an hour. The second required endurance plus skill: In 1915, a Captain Farrar, also English, took ten to one against his playing a standard golf course in fewer than one hundred strokes while wearing full infantry marching order, which included canteen, field kit and haversack. He shot a ninety-four.

Gluttony can legitimately be considered a form of endurance, can't it? Well, *Fine Bouche,* by Pierre Andrieu, tells about a Monsieur Choulot, the proprietor of a Paris restaurant called L'Ane Rouge: "Among his bets were some truly Gargantuan ones: to drink 100 bocks in a single day; to eat 100 oysters and 100 snails at a meal; to go up to the fifth floor of the Hôtel de la Cloche at Dijon, drinking a bottle of Burgundy at each landing.... He won all his bets without turning a hair."

Other bettors who fancied that their bellies were bottomless were tragically disillusioned. Of two London bricklayers who drank nearly three quarts of cherry brandy for a small wager, one died a few hours later.

A less dangerous challenge is to knock back twelve beers while Big Ben strikes noon—that is, in forty-three seconds. Richard Burton declared that he saw a man from Lancashire actually do it.

Enough of the physical. The bets that depend on wits, mental skill, are far more interesting. Consider Gerald Kersh's bet that he could write a short-short story exclusively in monosyllables (begging a few indispensable polysyllabic proper names) and sell it on its own merits, not merely as a *tour de force*. I have read the story: it's a good one. This is how it begins:

> We met on the stairs of time; I was on my way up; he was on his way down. I was young; he was old, and poor—so poor that he did not know when luck would send him a meal and a bed.

And so on for 1,561 words, all monosyllables but for *Hitler, Russia, Paris, Germany,* and one or two other such. (Robert Graves wrote a poem—though not on a bet—called "In Single Syllables": 159 of them and one bisyllable.)

Two of the cleverest bets I've found—or *sharpest,* if you prefer—have to do with horses. In the first a member of the Meadow Brook Club, on Long Island, bet that he could run the length of the polo field (300 yards) and back, on foot, before anyone else could ride the same course on a pony,

provided that the rider dismounted at the far end of the field and drank a glass of water before remounting and returning. Stipulations were that the pony not be lame, hobbled, ungovernable, or carrying a backbreaking impost and that the water not be polluted. The bet was taken. Which man won? The man on foot. The cunning devil saw to it that the water was boiling.

The other horse bet was proposed by a young fox hunter who had recently bought the "world's finest jumper," he boasted, and was prepared to back him against any other "for money or marbles." A friend accepted the bet but made one condition: that he is allowed to choose the obstacle. Agreed. At the showdown the friend laid *one straw* on the ground, rode up to it on a *blind horse,* and shouted, "Over! The horse obediently jumped, but neither whip nor spur could induce the "world's finest jumper" to leave the ground.

When I saw that the last bet in my collection was laid by Wilson Mizner, the legendary wit, prankster, and con man, you can expect chicanery—and you'll get it. According to his biographer, Alva Johnston, Mizner and some cronies were sauntering along the boardwalk at Atlantic City, idly betting "which of two sunbathers would be the first to go into the water or which of two swimmers would be the first to come out. One of the party noticed a pair of gigantic feet sticking out of a window on the first floor of a boardwalk hotel. . . . They began to guess how tall the man was. . . . Mizner made the lowest estimate: five feet one. When the money was up, they called on the man in the hotel room. He was a dwarf, four feet six inches tall, with No. 11 shoes." And now the snapper: Mizner had brought him from New York and planted him there.

Postscript: An early member of the English Jockey Club was one "Cripplegate" Barrymore, whose debauchery was "the scorn and wonder of his age." Before he shot himself, at twenty-four, he bet that he could eat a cat, *live*. I don't know whether he won or not. Queasiness kept me from reading further.

We Southerners

A visiting South Carolinian told his Boston host, "Just to hear myself talk makes me homesick."

Caskie Stinnett, a native of Fauquier County, Virginia: "Jimmy Carter was the first president we've had in years who didn't talk with an accent."

In April 1776, Captain Surman of the *New Shoreham*, having just been informed that war had been declared between Britain and the American colonies, expressed the opinion that "the Americans in general, especially those of the southern provinces, [were] the basest and most unprincipled people under the sun."

Memoirs of William Hickey,
edited by Peter Quennell

Lt. Colonel John S. Mosby, commanding the Forty-third Battalion, Virginia Partizan (*sic*) Rangers, to a new recruit: "I will tolerate no blasphemy or profanity in my command under any circumstances but one: when summoning an enemy to surrender, I permit you to call, 'Surrender, you Yankee son of a bitch!' "

Charlottesville, Va., 1865—The first election after The War.
A veteran of Stonewall Jackson's "foot cavalry" came down from the hills to vote and was dismayed to learn that he would first have to swear allegiance to the Union. He protested, but the registrar was firm: no oath, no vote. Grudgingly the veteran took it. Disconsolately he asked, "Does that make me a Yankee?"

"If you want to look at it that way."

The veteran's face brightened. He slapped the registrar's shoulder. "Boy!" he cried. "Didn't Old Jack lick hell out of us in the Valley of Virginia!"

The lower civilization, as represented by the South, is much braver and cunninger and daringer than the cultivated shopkeeper of the North. It is just as if the younger sons of the Irish and Scotch nobility were turned loose against the bourgeoisie of Leeds.

T. WEMYSS REED, *Life and Letters of Richard Monckton Milnes, Lord Houghton*

In 1824 one Samuel Taylor, a prominent citizen of Southside Virginia, was telling a friend that he had seen Lafayette. He added, "In his manners there is great simplicity. They must have been formed by the manners of the Virginia gentlemen with whom he associated in our Revolutionary War."

Quoted by HARRY COOPER, without source

Warrenton, Virginia, in the 1880s, one lady to another: "I simply can't understand why Martha Lou never got married. Her father had a *splendid* record in the war!"

Told by MRS. WALTER WILLIAMS

From a letter written me by an Alabama lady: "When my late father was 'weary and sore-oppressed,' he would suddenly shout, 'Robert E. Lee! Stonewall Jackson!' It seemed to hearten him. He explained, 'A man must have a rallying cry, something he can turn to for comfort and encouragement in times of trouble.'"

Don't confuse the Stars and Bars with the Confederate battle flag. The latter shows the Southern Cross. The former, the first flag adopted by the Confederate Congress, consists of three horizontal stripes—red, white, red—with a blue union and a wreath of white stars in the upper left corner.

Granddaddy Jenkins . . . never wore a blue shirt, or suit, or tie until he died, so great was his antipathy toward the Union.

DAVID H. HENDERSON,
Covey Rises and Other Pleasures

General Lee's horse, Traveller, was originally named Jefferson Davis.

What was Jefferson Davis's middle name? See the last word in the text of this book.

What Have These in Common?

(ANSWERS ON PAGES 305–306)

1. Queen Victoria, Napoleon, Victor Hugo, Richard III?
2. Poland, Canada, Turkey, Japan, Denmark, Switzerland, Peru, Monaco, Austria, Tunisia, Tonga, Laos, Yemen, Indonesia, Singapore, Bahrein?
3. Alembert, Paroli, Snowball, Tiers et Tout, Martingale, Labouchère ("Labby"), Anti-Labby, Beresford, Wells, Chaser, Avant Dernier?
4. Colombia, Liechtenstein, San Salvador, the Philippines, Rhodesia, Bolivia, Nicaragua?
5. Cambric, denim, lawn, lisle, muslin, poplin, worsted, jeans? All are woven fabrics, of course, but what else have they in common?
6. King George I of England, William Pitt the Younger, Thomas Moore, and Joseph Guillotin all were born on a May 28. Name five other well-known people who share this birthday.
7. The great Duke of Wellington; Sir Basil Zaharoff; Father Divine; Calouste Gulbenkian; Homer; George Psalmanazar, the French adventurer and impostor; Aristotle Onassis?
8. King William IV of England, Beau Brummell, the 1880s, London's street names, the President of Switzerland?
9. Charles Farrar Browne, David Ross Locke, Edgar Watson Nye, Henry Wheeler Shaw, Charles Henry Smith?
10. Pin, chat, dent, talon, sable, lit, loin, messes, main, pied, vague?
11. Moses; Sir Thomas Browne; St. John of God, founder of the Order of Charity; Sir Kenelm Digby, mathemati-

cian, warrior, philosopher, theologian; Ingrid Bergman; Humbert Wolfe, the English poet; Shakespeare; John Sobieski, King of Poland?

12. Silver, month, window, orange, plinth, false, depth, chimney, swamp?
13. Disraeli, Sir Thomas More, Shakespeare, W. H. Hudson, George Borrow (the author of *Lavengro*, etc.), Dr. Samuel Johnson, Robert Browning?
14. Connecticut, wretched, knives, Edinburgh, soften, psalmist, Wednesday, mnemonics, cupboard, faux pas?
15. Marshal Ney, Alfred Loewenstein, Jesus Christ, Ambrose Bierce, Nicholas II of Russia, Ivar Krueger, Rudolph Diesel, Amelia Earhart?
16. Covach, buckings, sollaghan, water souchy, oon, rumble-thumps, haps, snoodle, clod, claggum, fadge, blaaad?
17. George Taylor, James Smith, William Floyd, George Ross, Thomas Stone, James Wilson?
18. Lord De L'Isle and Lord Lyell? Their names are almost exact homonyms, and both went to Eton, but what else have they in common?
19. Evangeline Booth, Clara Barton, Isaac Newton, Steve Brodie, Gladys Swarthout, Rebecca West, Cab Calloway, Humphrey Bogart, Conrad Hilton, Tony Martin, "Believe It or Not" Ripley?
20. Lord Melbourne and Ramsay MacDonald, besides being prime ministers?
21. Janet Kent, Joseph Story, Asa Gray, Mary Lyon, Maria Mitchell, Joseph Henry, James Buchanan Eads, William Thomas Green Morton, Alice Freeman Palmer?
22. Jefferson Davis, Harry Greb, Tommy Armour, A. J. Munnings, Floyd Gibbons, Horatio Nelson, Wiley Post?
23. David Livingstone and the notorious Rector of Skiffkey?
24. Zane Grey and Doc Holliday, the drunken gambler who took part in the shoot-out at the OK Corral?
25. Albert Gallatin (born 1761) and C. Douglas Dillon born 1909), besides being U.S. Secretaries of the Treasury?

THINGS IN COMMON *(Answers)*

1. Each was born with one tooth.
2. Their national flags are red and white.
3. All are among the forty-odd different systems for winning at roulette.
4. All were named for persons; Nicarao was a local Indian chief.
5. All take their names from the places that specialized in weaving them: cambric, from Cambrai; denim is the *serge de Nîmes*; lawn, from Laon; lisle, from Lille; muslin, from Mosul, Iraq; poplin, from the *papal* town of Avignon; worsted, from Worstead, England; jeans, from Gênes, the French name of Genoa.
6. The Dionne quintuplets, born May 28, 1934.
7. It is not certain where any of them was born.
8. Sir Max Beerbohm found all of them "ridiculous."
9. All were famous American humorists in the nineteenth century. They were better known as, respectively, Artemus Ward, Petroleum V. Nasby, Bill Nye, Josh Billings, Bill Arp.
10. All are both English and French, though with different meanings in the different languages.
11. All died on their birthdays. Sobieski was also married and crowned on that day, June 17. Digby's birthday was also the date of the Battle of Scanderoon (1628), in which he fought heroically. His epitaph commemorates the coincidences:

    Under this tomb the matchless Digby lies,
    Digby the great, the valiant, and the wise;
    This age's wonder for his noble parts,
    Skilled in six tongues, and learned in all the arts;
    Born on the day he died, the eleventh of June,
    And that day bravely fought at Scanderoon;
    It's rare that one and the same day should be
    His day of birth, of death, of victory!

    The painter Raphael was born and died on Good Friday.
12. English has no rhyme for any of them.

13. Each married a woman considerably older than himself. (Viscount and Viscountess Astor, the former Nancy Langhorne, were exactly the same age, to the day.) The second husband of Queen Victoria's granddaughter "Young Vicky" was her junior by thirty-four years.
14. Each word has one or more silent letters.
15. It is not certain exactly how or when any of them died.
16. All are British provincial dishes, according to Richard Condon, writing in *Gourmet*.
17. All were signers of the Declaration of Independence.
18. They were the only peers to win the Victoria Cross in World War II.
19. All were born on Christmas Day.
20. Both were illegitimate.
21. All are enshrined in the U.S. Hall of Fame.
22. Each was blind in one eye.
23. Both were mauled by lions; the rector was killed.
24. Both practiced dentistry before they took up other professions.
25. Both were born in Geneva.

Which Is Which?

(ANSWERS ON NEXT PAGE)

1. Which of the Wright brothers made the first flight at Kitty Hawk, Wilbur or Orville?
2. Which is in the Northern Hemisphere, the Tropic of Cancer or the Tropic of Capricorn?
3. Which color on the French flag is next to the staff, the red or the blue?
4. Which is the right bank of a river as you face upstream, the left or the right?
5. Which had a red rose as its symbol, the House of Lancaster or the House of York?
6. Which of the Marx Brothers was the eldest, Groucho, Chico, or Harpo?
7. Which was the murdered pair in the famous Hall-Mills case (1926), Dr. Hall and Mrs. Mills or Dr. Mills and Mrs. Hall?
8. Which does *slumber* mean, "deep sleep" or "light doze"?
9. a) Which was the Confederate ironclad, the *Monitor* or the *Merrimack*?
   b) Which was the "cheesebox on a raft"?
10. Which had the moustache, Sacco or Vanzetti?
11. Which is the correct spelling, Barbara Freitchey, Frietchie, Friechey, or Frietchey?
12. Is Scylla a whirlpool and Charybdis a rock, or vice versa?
13. When driving mules or oxen, does *gee*! mean "Turn left!" and *haw*! "Turn right!" or vice versa?

WHICH IS WHICH? *(Answers)*

1. Orville.
2. The Tropic of Cancer.
3. Blue.
4. The left.
5. Lancaster.
6. Chico, born in 1891; Harpo was born in 1893 and Groucho in 1895.
7. Dr. Hall and Mrs. Mills.
8. Light doze.
9. a) *Merrimack*.
   b) *Monitor*.
10. Vanzetti.
11. Frietchie.
12. Vice versa.
13. Vice versa.

Words

An English-speaking person of average education has a vocabulary approximately 43 times the number of words he knows that begin with the letter O.

LOUIS SOBOL

Contradictions in terms: Little Big Horn, pianoforte, bittersweet, Fork Union, Old New York.

Taxicab (O marvelous, ill-made word, surely the password somewhere of some evil order).

LORD DUNSANY, *"The Beggars"*

Words that I am impatient to drop into the conversation:

Quaquaversal: turning or dipping in any or every direction (see Foreword).

Shonsified: pleased with oneself.

Ataraxia: peace of mind, detached serenity.

Hypergamy: marrying a woman above one's station.

The word *bankrupt* was once printed *b - - - - - pt*, as though it were profane or obscene.

The longest one-word palindrome I ever saw is SAIPPUAKAUPPIAS, which means "soap salesman" in Finnish.

The longest English words that can be written on a single row of typewriter keys are *perpetuity, proprietor*, *prerequire*, and *typewriter*.

Word Quiz

(ANSWERS ON NEXT PAGE)

1. Name a word for which Webster authorizes six different pronunciations.
2. How many 5-letter words can you make from *residuals*? No past tenses allowed and no plurals.
3. Fit each of these groups of letters into an English word: *ILIW, ILIL.*
4. Name a word containing five successive vowels.
5. Six successive consonants.

6a. A 4-letter word with 5 anagrams.

6b. A 4-letter word with 6 anagrams.

7. Pronounce *minuscule*, *harass*, *contumely*, *prothonotary*, and *Cibber* (English poet laureate).
8. A word with:
   a. double *u*'s
   b. 3 *u*'s
   c. 3 *y*'s
   d. 4 *a*'s
   e. 4 *o*'s
   f. 4 *i*'s
   g. 5 *e*'s
   h. 3 *successive e*'s
9. What word can you prefix to each of a pair of adjectives of opposite meaning (e.g., light-dark, open-shut, alive-dead) to make their meanings the same?
10. Name a word with two opposed meanings, according to how it is pronounced.
11. What are the opposites of *whip hand, feudal, squaw,* and *distaff side*?

WORD QUIZ *(Answers)*

1. Hegemony. The first *e* may be long or short; the *g*, either hard or soft; and the accent may be on either the first or second syllable.
2. at least thirty-three:

   aider
   aisle
   alder
   arise
   aside

   dares
   deals
   dials
   dress
   dries
   duels

   ideal
   idler

   laser
   lauds
   leads
   lures
   lurid

   rails
   raise
   rides
   riles
   rises
   rules

   sails
   seals
   serai
   sides
   sidle
   sires
   slade
   slide
   slues

3. bailiwick, oilily
4. miaoued. Also *shuyuaeiet*, "a female Communist" in Arabic.
5. latchstring, eschscholtzia. According to *The World Mine Oyster*, by Matila Ghyka, there is a Balkan soup called *schtschi—seven* successive consonants.
6. a. live, levi, evil, vile, veil
   b. stop, post, pots, opts, spot, tops
7. mi-NUS-cule, HAR-ass, CON-tumely, pro-THON-otary, KIB-ber
8. a. vacuum, residuum
   b. unusual
   c. syzygy
   d. Alabama, Madagascar
   e. hoodoo, voodoo
   f. Philistinism
      Mississippi
      inspiriting

inhibiting
primitivism

g. resweetened
h. créée— the feminine past participle of the French *créer* (I admit that this is unfair).

9. half
10. im-*pugn'*-able: assailable; im-*pug'*-nable: unassailable; an-a-the'-ma: an offering to a divinity; a-*nath'*-e-ma: a ban or curse
11. rein hand, alodial, sannup, spear side

Writers

I believe that nothing completely satisfies an imaginative writer but copious and continuous draughts of unmitigated praise, always provided it is accompanied by a large and increasing sale of his works.

FREDERICK LOCKER-LAMPSON, *My Confidences*

I have read that the Rev. C. R. Maturin [the author of Gothic novels], when in the throes of composition, used to be seen with a red wafer stuck on his forehead, a sign to his numerous family that he was not to be spoken to.

IB.

Tom Campbell, who was a fastidious writer [and author of "Hohenlinden," "Lord Ullin's Daughter," etc.], once took a six-mile walk to his printer (and six back again) to see a comma changed into a semicolon.

IB.

My repugnance to the writing table becomes daily and hourly more deadly and insurmountable. In place of this has come a canine appetite for reading.

THOMAS JEFFERSON

Evelyn Waugh thought that anyone could write a novel given six weeks, pen, paper and no telephone or wife.

Chips: The Diaries of Sir Henry Channon

Write the things which thou has seen and the things which are and the things which shall be hereafter.

Revelation 1:19

The path to an author's heart: "Now that I've actually met you, I must read your new book! I saw a copy at my sister's, and I'm sure she'll let me skim it before she returns it to the library."

Alternatively: "My friends are *standing in line* to borrow my copy of your new book!"

Bram Stoker, the author of *Dracula*, also wrote a factual book, *Famous Imposters*. According to a legend (which Stoker accepts), one of his imposters, "the Bisley boy," was substituted for Henry VIII's daughter Princess Elizabeth, who died in childhood; and the boy reigned as "Queen Elizabeth." (The strange name "Bram" was a condensation of Stoker's real name, "Abraham.")

An author who sent Richard Brinsley Sheridan a copy of his new book, hoping for a quotable puff, usually was sent this in return: "I have received your book and no doubt shall be delighted after I have read it." Disraeli's acknowledgment was equally ambiguous: "I thank you for your book. I shall lose no time in reading it."

Famous author to adoring young thing: "But let's not talk about *me* any more. Let's talk about *you*. Tell me, what did you think of my new book?"

Punch cartoon, in the 1920s

Whole poems have been constructed for the eye by a technique called technopaegnia. The inventor of this form is said to have been the Greek poet Theodoric, who composed poems shaped like axes, bottles, eggs and frying pans.

NOAH JONATHAN JACOBS, *Naming-Day in Eden.*
(A familiar example is "The Mouse's Tale," in *Alice in Wonderland.*)

Imbeciles are writing the lives of other imbeciles every day.

AGATHA CHRISTIE, *Poirot Loses a Client*

Where burning Sappho loved and sung.

BYRON, *Don Juan*

It only leaves me fifty more.

A. E. HOUSMAN, *A Shropshire Lad*

Byron needed the *sung-sprung* rhyme, so he had an excuse, though feeble, for his bad grammar. But I see no reason for Housman not to have written, correctly, "It leaves me only fifty more."

Prolificity:
Edward Z. C. Judson, who wrote the "Buffalo Bill" stories under the name of "Ned Buntline," once turned out

a 600-page novel in sixty-two hours. Col. Prentiss Ingraham, who took up the series when Judson left off, wrote a 35,000-word novel in a day. There are 773,692 words in the Bible. Gilbert Patten, author of the 776 "Frank Merriwell" books, wrote an equivalent wordage every four months—more than 6,000 words a day, *every* day; his total for seventeen years was 35,000,000 words. Mrs. Frances Trollope, mother of Anthony Trollope and author of the offensive *Domestic Manners of the Americans* (1852), wrote 115 novels between the age of fifty and her death at eighty-three.

Ellen Glasgow, author of *The Romantic Comedians* and other fine novels, wore gloves while she was typing.

Thackeray's description of King George IV's prose style: "Lax, maudlin slipslop."

Unprovided with original learning, unformed in the habits of thinking, unskilled in the arts of composition, I resolved to write a book.

EDWARD GIBBON

Ernest Hemingway's middle name was Miller, and Jefferson Davis's was

FINIS

About the Author

J. (for "Joseph") Bryan, III, was born in Richmond, Virginia, in 1904. He graduated from Princeton in 1927, traveled in Russia, Persia and East Africa, and returned home, briefly, to write editorials and features for the *Richmond News Leader.* He left Richmond again in 1932 to work on first the *Chicago Journal*, then *Time, Fortune, Parade* (Cleveland), *The New Yorker, Town and Country* (as managing editor), and finally *The Saturday Evening Post* (as associated editor). He resigned from the *Post* in 1940 to become a freelance and has been one ever since. His articles have appeared in all the major American magazines, and he has written many books, including *The Windsor Story* (in collaboration with Charles J. V. Murphy), which was a main selection with the Book-of-the-Month Club, and, most recently, *Merry Gentlemen* (*and One Lady*). After serving in the Army (1st lieutenant), Navy (lieutenant commander), and Air Force (colonel), Bryan returned to Richmond for good in 1959, and lives there in a house built by his great-great-great-grandfather.